S0-BRG-709

# MEMORIES OF A
# MUSICAL LIFE

Da Capo Press Music Reprint Series

GENERAL EDITOR

FREDERICK FREEDMAN

VASSAR COLLEGE

# MEMORIES OF A MUSICAL LIFE

By William Mason

𝄘 DA CAPO PRESS · NEW YORK · 1970

A Da Capo Press Reprint Edition

This Da Capo Press edition of
*Memories of a Musical Life*
is an unabridged republication of the
first edition published in New York in 1901.

*Library of Congress Catalog Card Number 70-125056*

SBN 306-70021-2

Published by Da Capo Press
A Division of Plenum Publishing Corporation
227 West 17th Street, New York, N.Y. 10011

MEMORIES OF A
MUSICAL LIFE

WILLIAM MASON IN 1899

Memories of a
Musical Life
by
William Mason

NEW YORK
THE CENTURY CO.
MCMI

# CONTENTS

vii

# CONTENTS

PAGE

The author acknowledges the efficient collaboration of Mr. Gustav Kobbé in preparing these Memories for publication, and also the valuable assistance of his son-in-law, Mr. Howard van Sinderen.

# LIST OF ILLUSTRATIONS

xi

MEMORIES
OF A MUSICAL LIFE

# MEMORIES
# OF A MUSICAL LIFE

❧

## EARLY DAYS IN NEW ENGLAND

I AM the third son of Lowell Mason of Medfield, Massachusetts, and of Abigail Gregory of Westborough, Massachusetts, his wife, and I was born in Boston on January 24, 1829. My father was in the seventh generation from Robert Mason, who was born in England about the year 1590. In 1630 Robert came to America, and was probably one of John Winthrop's company, landing at Salem on the twelfth day of June of that year. Thomas Mason, the elder son of Robert, went to Medfield to live in the second year of the settlement of the town. His marriage with Margery Partridge, on April 23, 1653, was the first marriage to be entered upon

3

the town records; and the homestead lands, which he acquired by grant from the town, have ever since remained in possession of some member of the Mason family. Thomas and two of his sons were killed by the Indians under Monaco on February 21, 1676, when Medfield was burned. The line was continued through Ebenezer, a third son, born at Medfield, September 12, 1669; Thomas, a son of Ebenezer, born at Medfield, April 23, 1699; Barachias, son of Thomas, born at Medfield, June 10, 1723, who was musical and who taught singing; and Johnson, son of Barachias, born at Medfield, August 7, 1767. Johnson was the father of Lowell Mason, who was born at Medfield, January 8, 1792. On January 8, 1892, the one hundredth anniversary of my father's birth was celebrated at Medfield, under the auspices of the Historical Society of that place. In the address delivered by the president of the society, a period of his life was touched upon concerning which but little had heretofore been pub-lished. The address will be interesting to

those who are interested in him and in
the work which he accomplished, and is
printed, by permission, in an appendix to
these memories.

The difference between Boston and New
York as musical centers is largely due to
my father. He made Boston a self-developing musical city. New York has
received its musical culture from abroad.

My father manifested a remarkable
fondness for music at an early age. His
parents did not intend that he should
take up music as a profession, but his
talent was not neglected. In 1812, before he was twenty, he heard of an opening in a bank in Savannah, Georgia, and
having secured the position, he went
there. After business hours he continued
his studies in music with an instructor
named F. L. Abel, under whom he made
rapid progress. He soon attempted composition, his first efforts being hymn-tunes
and anthems. He arranged a collection
consisting of a group of selections from
William Gardiner's "Sacred Melodies,"
to which he added some of his own com-

positions. For this collection he vainly
endeavored to find a publisher in Phila-
delphia and Boston, until chance brought
to Savannah a Boston organ-builder,
W. M. Goodrich, who had come to set up
an organ. He induced my father to go to
Boston in person, with the result that the
work was submitted to Dr. G. K. Jackson,
the organist of the Handel and Haydn
Society, and received his approval. It
was published in 1822, with the title, "The
Boston Handel and Haydn Society's Collection of Music," and was an instant success, finding its way into singing-schools
and church choirs throughout New England. Some of my father's hymn-tunes
have become famous. It has been said
that his missionary hymn, "From Green-
land's Icy Mountains," has been sung in
more languages than any other sacred
tune. Among the many popular tunes
which he composed are "Boylston,"
"Hebron," "Olivet," and "Bethany"; and
one of his collections of sacred melodies
brought him in over a hundred thousand
dollars in royalties.

## LOWELL MASON'S CAREER

THE success of my father's first venture led him to leave Savannah and settle in Boston. Then, as now, the Handel and Haydn Society was largely recruited from church choirs, but in those days its concerts were few, and these were almost entirely devoted to church music. Rarely was a "work" offered to the public. Outside the realm of church music, the society's repertory consisted of "The Messiah," "The Creation" (and more frequently fragments from these), the "Dettingen Te Deum" by Handel, and the "Intercession" by M. P. King, who has long since been forgotten. For five years my father was president of the society, and served as musical director, the special employment of a conductor not having been authorized until 1847.

Meanwhile he was constantly aiming at the introduction of popular education in music. It was through his efforts—and strenuous efforts they were—that music was introduced into the Boston public schools. To bring this about he first taught classes of children free of charge, and gave concerts to illustrate the practicability of his plans. When finally musical education was made a part of the Boston public-school system, the city council refused to make any appropriation for it, and he served as instructor for a year gratuitously, beginning work in 1837 in the Hawes Grammar School, South Boston. The experiment was a complete success. Music was generally introduced into the public schools, and my father was made superintendent of the department. The seeds he sowed then are still bearing fruit. This was part of his labor which created in Boston a self-developing musical activity. While Dr. Samuel G. Howe was engaged in organizing the Perkins Institution for the Blind in 1832, at his request my father devised a system of musical instruction for the blind.

### FIRST BEETHOVEN SYMPHONY
### IN AMERICA

ABOUT 1830 an English musician, Mr. George James Webb, settled in Boston.

He was a gentleman of high culture, thoroughly educated in music, played the organ well, and was a good vocal teacher. His talents and his personal charm were promptly recognized. My father became intimate with him, and in 1833, with the coöperation of certain influential gentlemen of Boston, they founded the Boston Academy of Music, my father taking charge of the special department of church music, while Mr. Webb devoted himself chiefly to secular music and voice-culture. Instrumental concerts were also given at the academy, and there, on February 10, 1841, occurred the first performance in America of a Beethoven symphony, the Fifth, which was played by an orchestra of twenty-three, under the direction of Henry Schmidt.

### MUSICAL CONVENTIONS

MY father originated the idea of assembling music-teachers in classes. In 1838, when the experiment was not more than three years old, one hundred and thirty-four teachers, representing ten States, assembled at the academy. From these assemblages grew the musical conventions which my father held throughout New England and in some of the other States. Choir-singers and other musically inclined people from the towns lying within the surrounding district would gather at a central point, and he would hold a musical convention lasting for several days, drilling the singers in church music, but also, where he found sufficient advancement, in music of a higher order. The Worcester festivals may be traced to these conventions.

### EARLY MUSICAL TRAINING

I HAD shown my fondness for music at a very early age. When I was a child, my father was the organist of the Bowdoin Street Congregational Church in Boston, of which Lyman Beecher had been the pastor. When I was seven years old, he placed me unexpectedly on the organ-bench at a public service, and while the choir sang the tune of "Boylston," I played the accompaniment. Up to this time I had had but little instruction in pianoforte-playing. My mother used to sit by me and guide me in the way of careful practising, and thus I had acquired considerable facility for those days, though now I have a feeling of compassion for any one who had to listen to me.

I became useful to my father as an accompanist, and when he went to musical conventions he took me along with him, and I would play the piano accompaniments while he conducted.

## WEBSTER AND CLAY

IT was at about this time that my father took me with him on a trip to Providence. In those days the entrance to the cars was from the side, and we took seats nearly opposite the door. My father called my attention to a very dignified and impressive-looking man in the front corner of the car, saying : "William, the gentleman in the corner is Daniel Webster. Go over and wish him good morning." I promptly obeyed, and marching over to him, said, "Good morning, Daniel Webster." He asked my name, and I replied, saying my father was "over there," and then he exchanged greetings with my father. I was somewhat awed by his great dignity, and remember very well his piercing eyes.

About the year 1842 I went to Maysville, Kentucky, to stay with the family of my uncle, Mr. E. F. Tucker. My health had not been good, and the change of residence was thought to be judicious. My uncle was at the head of some factory in Maysville, and one day, after I had been there for some time, a gentleman called at the house to see him about business connected with the factory. My aunt called me, and, presenting me to the gentleman, requested me to show him the way to the factory. This gentleman was Henry Clay. I remember his urbanity, and his friendly conversation attracted me. This time it was not the eye which was noticeable, but the mouth, which was unusually large.

WILLIAM MASON AS A BOY

FROM A DAGUERREOTYPE

### FIRST PUBLIC APPEARANCE

RETURNING to Boston after a year, I was
sent to Newport, Rhode Island, to study
under the Rev. T. T. Thayer, who was a
Congregational clergyman in that place.
In a short time after my arrival I
began playing the organ at the services
in his church, and continued this with
regularity until my return to Boston a
few years later.  At Boston I became the
organist at the Congregational church in
Winter street, at which my father was
music-conductor.

I played in public about the year 1846,
in one of the concerts of the Boston
Academy of Music, given in the Odeon,
which was then the principal concert-hall
in Boston.  On this occasion I had the
accompaniment of a string quartet.  This
was my first regular appearance in public.
About this time, too, I began taking
pianoforte lessons of Mr. Henry Schmidt,
to whom reference has been made as the
conductor of Beethoven's "Fifth Symphony" on the occasion of the first per-

formance of this work in Boston. Mr. Schmidt's instrument was the violin, but he was also an excellent pianoforte teacher, and to his careful and skilful instruction I owe very much. I remember that in those days I was more fond of playing—if my habit of improvising in a loose or inaccurate way can be so called —than of careful practising and close attention to detail. When my lesson-hour arrived I used to trust much to luck, and thus occasioned poor Mr. Schmidt a deal of trouble and vexation. He begged and entreated me to be careful, and after a while a spirit of contrition overcame me, and so, on a certain occasion, I really did practise carefully and to my best ability during the interval between my lessons. When Mr. Schmidt made his appearance, however, I became so nervous and apprehensive lest my work should not show to advantage that the very thing I dreaded took place, and I stumbled through my piece in a distressing manner. I do not wonder that my teacher's patience was tried, and he rebuked me with severity,

saying that he believed I had not practised at all since the previous lesson.    I
received this all very meekly, but when
he took his departure I pitched the music
into a corner, and did not practise until
he made his appearance for the following
lesson.    At this lesson, however, I played
with great accuracy and spirit, much to
my gratification and somewhat to my
surprise.    Mr. Schmidt warmly com-
mended my work, and attributed it to
the fact that I had *now* practised indus-
triously and carefully.    I had enough
sense to know that the successful result
was owing to the practice I had previously done, and which needed time to
produce its results.    This bit of experience I commend to pianoforte students for
careful consideration, to show that acts
are not always immediately followed by
desirable results.

Mr. Schmidt taught me much concerning the production of tone in pianoforte
playing, and in particular led me to acquire a certain habit of touch which I
have never lost, and which has been the

means of greatly lessening the fatigue
which would otherwise have been attendant on the performance of pieces which
require much strength and long-continued
endurance. I write somewhat at length
concerning this matter, feeling that a
knowledge of my experience may be of
substantial use to pianoforte students.

The habit referred to has especial relation to the playing of the various rapid
scale and arpeggio passages, involving
closed or open hand position which are so
common in pianoforte compositions and
which grow out of the nature of the instrument. The touch is accomplished by
quickly but quietly drawing the finger-
tips inward toward the palm of the hand,
or, in other words, slightly and partly
closing the finger-points as they touch
the keys while playing. This action of
the fingers secures the coöperation of
many more muscles of the finger, wrist,
hand, and forearm than could be accomplished by the merely "up-and-down"
finger-touch. It is difficult to describe
in detail without an instrument at hand

for illustration. If correctly performed, however, the tones produced are very clear and well defined, and of a beautifully musical quality. The simile of "a string of pearls" of precisely similar size and shape has often been used in describing their fluency and clearness of outline. A too rapid withdrawal of the finger-tips would result in a short and crisp staccato. While this extreme staccato is also desirable and frequently used, it is not the kind of effect here desired, namely, a clear, clean delivery of the tones which in no wise disturb the legato effect.

Of course it requires cultivation and skill to secure just the right degree of finger-motion to preserve the legato and at the same time the slight separation of each tone. Therefore the fingers must not be drawn so quickly as to produce a separation or staccato effect, but in just the right degree to avoid impairing the legato or binding effect. For the sake of convenience in description I have named this touch the "elastic finger-touch," and through its influence a clear and crisp

effect is attained.    It is interesting to
observe in this connection, a fact which I
learned only many years later, that Sebastian Bach's touch, described in detail
by J. N. Forkel in his work entitled
"Über Johann Sebastian Bachs Leben,
Kunst und Kunstwerke," both as used by
Bach himself and as he taught it to his
pupils, seems to be identical with the
touch I am here attempting to describe.
Forkel expressly emphasizes the "pulling-
in" motion of the finger-tips.    While it
has relation solely to finger-action as distinguished from the action of the wrist
and arm, it cannot be accomplished
properly without bringing into action the
flexor and extensor muscles, principally
of the forearm from wrist to elbow.

Through the medium of this touch
pianissimo effects are possible which no
other mechanism can reach, for passages
of the most extreme delicacy and softness
still retain the quality of vitality and
clearness of outline.

During the season of 1846 I played the
pianoforte part throughout the series of

six concerts of chamber-music given by
the Harvard Musical Association. I remember that Mr. Blessner played the
violin and Mr. Groenvelt the violoncello,
but cannot recall the names of the players
of the second violin and viola. These
concerts were given at the pianoforte
warerooms of Mr. Jonas Chickering, 334
Washington street, Boston. I still have
the programs. String quartets by Haydn,
Mozart, and Beethoven were played, also
piano trios by Beethoven, Reissiger, and
Mayseder.

### LEOPOLD DE MEYER

THE knowledge I gained from Mr.
Schmidt was largely advanced and sup-
plemented by what I learned a year or
two later, in 1847–48, from the playing of
the pianoforte virtuoso Leopold de Meyer,
who came to the United States about that
time.

It was from a careful study of the manner of his playing that I first acquired the
habit of fully devitalized upper-arm muscles in pianoforte-playing. The loveli-

ness and charming musical beauty of his tones, the product of these conditions, greatly excited my admiration and fascinated me. I never missed an opportunity of hearing him play, and closely watched his movements, and particularly the motions of hand, arm, and shoulder. I was incessantly at the pianoforte trying to produce the same delightful tone quality by imitating his manner and style.

My continued perseverance was rewarded with success, for the result was a habit of devitalized muscular action in such degree that I could practically play all day without a feeling of fatigue. The constant alternation between devitalization and reconstruction keeps the muscles always fresh for their work and enables the player to rest while playing. The force is so distributed that each and every muscle has ample opportunity to rest while yet in a state of activity. Furthermore the tones resulting from this touch are sonorous and full of energy and life. An idea of my own which was persistently carried into act aided materially in bring-

WILLIAM MASON AT THE AGE OF EIGHTEEN
FROM A DAGUERREOTYPE

ing about the desired result.   This was to
allow the arms to hang limp by my side,
either in a sitting or standing posture,
and then to shake them vigorously with
the utmost possible looseness and devitalization.    This device was in after years
recommended to my pupils, and those
who persistently followed it up and per-
severed for a while gained great advantage from it, and eventually acquired a
state of habitual muscular elasticity and
flexibility.

I might easily have learned from any
book of anatomy the names of the muscles which are here referred to, but for
the practical instruction of pianoforte
pupils this seemed to be of little consequence.  However, there are three muscles
of the upper arm which may here be
named : the triceps, the brachialis anticus,
and the biceps.    Of these the first-named
is of the most importance to the pianist.

Leopold de Meyer's New York concerts
were given in the old Broadway Taber-
nacle, some distance below Canal street,
as I now remember.    The piano-lovers

were not so numerous then as they are now, and it was difficult to fill the hall, even with the help of deadheads. De Meyer's agent, acting on the principle that "a crowd draws a crowd," hired a lot of carriages to make their appearance a little before the concert-hour, and to stand in front of the doors and then advance in turn, so that passers-by might receive the impression of activity on the part of the concert-goers.

### "FATHER HEINRICH"

SOMEWHERE about this time there lived in New York an elderly German musician and composer who had somehow gained the cognomen of "Father Heinrich." He composed quite a number of large works, both vocal and instrumental, and also a number of pianoforte pieces. During a visit which he made to Boston, his headquarters were at Chickering's pianoforte warerooms, and on one occasion I was presented to him as a youth of some musical promise. He immediately showed me one of his pianoforte pieces in manuscript, and said : "Young man, I am going to test your musical talent and intelligence and see if you appreciate in any degree the importance of a proper observance of dynamics in musical interpretation." He had placed the open pages of the manuscript on the pianoforte desk, and I was glancing over them in close scrutiny. "I wish to tell you before you begin to play that I have submitted this piece to two or three of the best musicians in New York and they have failed to bring out the intended effect in an important phrase." This remark put me at once on my guard, and while he was talking I was closely scrutinizing the manuscript to see if there was some dynamic or other mark which would reveal his intention. About half-way down the second page I discovered a series of sforzando marks, thus : $> > > > >$ over several notes in one of the inner parts, and immediately determined to bring out these tones with all possible force. Further than this there seemed to be no peculiarity ; but as he had by this time finished his remarks I began to play with special care. The piece was easy to read, and so I made good progress, and on coming to the passage referred to I put a tremendous emphasis on the tones marked sforzando, playing all of the other voices by contrast quite softly. To my boyish satisfaction I found I had hit the mark. The excitement and pleasure of Father Heinrich was excessive and amusing. "Bravo! bravo!" he cried. "You have great talent, and you have done what none of our musicians in New York have accomplished!"

I did not at the time understand how he could lay so much stress on the affair, but in the light of a long experience as teacher of the pianoforte I no longer wonder at his excitement. All music is full of nuances and accents of greater or less intensity, to which pupils hardly ever give any attention, although they are necessary in order to give due expression to rhythm. They correspond to vocal accents in reading aloud, or in declamation.

AN EMBARRASSING EXPERIENCE

It is difficult to realize the crudity of
musical taste in the early days. I remember that in 1840 my father conducted
a convention in Vermont—I think in
Woodstock. We went by rail as far as
we could, and then traveled a number of
hours by coach. We were received by
the dignitaries of the town, and conducted
to the house in which we were to stay.
While we were shaking off the dust of
travel, we heard the sounds of drum and
fife. Looking out of the window, we
found that these instruments headed a
small procession which had come to escort
us to the church. The drum and the fife
were the instrumental outfit of the town ;
so, led by these, my father and I marched
with the magnates of the place to the
church. I still remember how foolish I
felt.

In 1846 my father was preparing to hold
a convention in Augusta, Maine. Mr.
Webb was to go with him, and I was sent
to his house the evening before they were

to start to let him know about the arrangements.    Though I knew Mr. Webb
very well, I had never had occasion to go
to his house.    At this time I was seventeen
years old.    When I was shown into the
drawing-room, I saw Mr. and Mrs. Webb
and their daughter, a girl then not four-
teen.    I had not been in the house half
an hour before I was deeply in love with
her.    I found that she was going to Augusta, and I decided at once that I would
go, too.    So the next day we all started
together.    She and I grew to be good
friends, but the idea of an engagement
between us was not to be thought of at
that time, and while I lived in Germany
we were not permitted to correspond.
For five years I did not see her ; but when
I came back I hastened to her father's
house.    The sequel I shall tell later.

## STUDENT LIFE ABROAD

IT having been decided that I should continue my musical studies in Europe, I sailed from New York for Bremen on the side-wheel steamer *Herrmann* in May, 1849, accompanied by Mr. Frank Hill of Boston, who had already attained some distinction as a pianist. My intention was to go directly to Leipsic to study with Moscheles. One of our fellow-passengers was Julius Schuberth, the music-publisher of Hamburg, who had been in America on business. Arriving at Bremen, we learned that the insurrection had not yet been suppressed, and that within two or three days there had been bloodshed in the streets of Leipsic. For this and other reasons I gladly accepted Mr. Schuberth's invitation to visit him, first making a short trip to Paris with Hill.

### MEETING WITH MEYERBEER

I ARRIVED in Paris shortly after six o'clock in the morning, and went to the Hôtel de Paris, in the Rue de Richelieu. In those days, at that early hour, Paris was as quiet as an American town at midnight. There were three of us in the party. We secured two rooms, and my friends remained up-stairs, while I returned to the porter's lodge below to have my passport sent to the Bureau of Police to be viséd. The porter went out to attend to this, and I was left alone in the lodge.

Shortly afterward a man entered, of medium height, well dressed, and with a good deal of manner. He addressed me in French, but when I asked him if he could speak English he began conversing fluently in that language. He asked if I was from England and a stranger in Paris. When I told him I was from America, he exclaimed, "Ah, that is farther off." Then, noticing the passport, which was uncommonly large and was bound like a book, he asked, "Is that an American passport? Please let me have a look at it. I 'm curious to see it." Bound in with the passport were a number of blank leaves to be used for the visés of various consuls. "Young man," said my chance acquaintance, "you have leaves enough there to travel about Europe for twenty years." Then he inquired if I was traveling for pleasure or on business.

"I have come over to study music."

"Ah, composition?"

"No ; mainly piano, but also theory and composition."

"And where?"

"I expect to go to Leipsic to study with Moscheles, Hauptmann, and Richter. Eventually I hope to go to Liszt."

"Well, well, you 've chosen good men. Moscheles knew Beethoven."

Then, with a few friendly words, he left the lodge and entered the hotel. Just as he was leaving the porter returned.

"Who is the gentleman?" I asked, pointing after the disappearing form.

"Meyerbeer, the composer."

The porter then took me into the court-
yard and pointed out the room which
Meyerbeer occupied, calling my attention
to the fact that his window and mine
almost faced each other.

"If you look out of your window about
eleven o'clock," said the porter, "you will
see Mme. Garcia and Roger, the tenor,
coming here to rehearse their rôles in the
new opera with the composer."

Meyerbeer was so affable at our chance
meeting that I think I could easily have
followed it up and have seen more of him ;
but when a boy is in Paris for the first
time, he has many things to think of.
Moreover, I did not realize that at the
end of the century, "Le Prophète," the
work which Meyerbeer was then rehearsing, would still be in the repertory of
every first-class opera-house.  I knew that
he was a distinguished composer, but I did
not for a moment imagine that his work
would live so long.   As I now look back
through the perspective of time, I realize
the  opportunity  I  missed ; but I thank
the freak  of  fortune  which  threw in his

way, if only for a few moments, a young man who was too careless to improve the chance acquaintance.

From Paris I returned to Schuberth's in Hamburg. He was an active, enterprising, pushing business man, with a large acquaintance in the musical world, and the knowledge of how to put it to the best use. I remained in Hamburg for some time. Boy-like, I had spent all my money in Paris, and was now obliged to wait for a remittance from home. In Hamburg I met Carl Mayer of Dresden, a fine pianist of the Hummel school, and Mortier de Fontaine, who was very well known in his day as a Beethoven-player —had, in fact, won considerable fame as the first pianist to perform Beethoven's "Sonata, Op. 106" in public. That was his label.

### LISZT'S FEAT OF MEMORY

FROM Hamburg I went to Leipsic, but Schuberth did not lose sight of me. Whenever he came there he looked me up, and was very kind in introducing me to people whom it was well for me to meet. He knew Liszt very well, and having taken a fancy to a composition of mine, "Les Perles de Rosée," which was still in manuscript, he said : "Let me have it for publication. Dedicate it to Liszt. I can easily get Liszt to accept the dedication. I am going directly from here to Weimar, and will see him about it. At the same time, I will prepare the way for your reception later as a pupil."

Not long afterward I received a letter from Schuberth in which he told me that when he handed the music to Liszt, the latter looked at the manuscript, hummed it over, then sat down and played it from memory. Then, going to his desk, he took a pen, and accepted the dedication by writing his name at the top of the title-page. Encouraged by this, I wrote a letter to Liszt, expressing my desire to become one of his pupils, and asking what my chances were. Unfortunately, I misinterpreted his reply, and received the impression that it amounted to a re-

Exercice
Allegro
p cres - cen - do
ten
ten
Leipzig den 8ten Februar 1850.
J. Moscheles

fusal; but at the same time he gave me a cordial invitation to attend the festival about to take place in Weimar in commemoration of the hundredth anniversary of Goethe's birth. I still have this letter, which is dated August 18, 1849. Had I understood then that Liszt was ready to accept me as a pupil, I should have taken up my residence at Weimar at once, instead of waiting until I learned my mistake, as I did during a call which I made upon Liszt nearly four years later.

### FIRST MEETING WITH LISZT

However, I went to Weimar with Mr. Hill to attend the Goethe festival, arriving there early in the afternoon of the day before it began.

The third day of the festival we called on Liszt, who was then living in the Hotel zum Erbprinzen, and were received most cordially. Schlesinger, the Paris publisher, was there with his little daughter, who was precocious as a pianist and played several Chopin waltzes. Liszt

was very busy with his guests, so that
our visit was limited, and nothing was
said about my coming to Weimar to study
except that Liszt said he never received
pupils for regular lessons, but that those
who lived in Weimar (and there were
only three or four in those days) had
frequent opportunities of hearing and
meeting artists who visited him.  Having
misinterpreted his letter, I accepted these
remarks as a further politely worded re-
fusal to receive me.  So I returned to
Leipsic to continue my studies there.

## ARRIVAL AT LEIPSIC

I WELL remember the feeling of awe mingled with interest with which I looked
upon every German whom I met in the
streets of Leipsic on my first arrival in
that famously musical city.  I looked on
even the laboring-men, the peasants as
well as those in higher positions, as being
Mozarts and Beethovens, and the idea
gained such ascendancy that I felt my
own inferiority and metaphorically held

down my head. This feeling, however, was not of long duration, and changed in the course of a month or two on account of what happened at a concert of the Euterpe Society which I attended. The concerts of this musical society were second only to those of the famous Gewandhaus, and their audiences were made up largely of those who attended the concerts of the latter. At this concert the program was classical and unimpeachable as to the orchestral concerted pieces, but one of the numbers was a solo for clarinet. At my age I was disposed to look down on this as an inferior kind of music, and as decidedly unsuitable to an educated and musically cultivated taste. Therefore, when, to my surprise, this turned out to be the most popular piece of the evening and received the most vociferous applause of the entire audience, I found my high opinion of the select musical taste of the Germans sensibly decreased.

Since then I have learned that there is a place for everything good in its way; but the clarinet solo seemed out of place in the classical atmosphere of a symphony concert.

### MOSCHELES, BEETHOVEN, AND CHOPIN

MOSCHELES, with whom I studied in Leipsic, had been a pupil of Dionysius Weber in Prague. At that time Beethoven was still a newcomer, and was regarded with skepticism by the older men, whose ideas were formed and who could not get over their first unfavorable impressions of him. Beethoven was a profound man and had strong individuality. He was eagerly accepted by the younger men, Moscheles among them; but Dionysius Weber regarded him as a monstrosity, and would never allow Moscheles to learn any of his music. Consequently, Moscheles practised Beethoven in secret, and when he grew up he prided himself on being a Beethoven-player, and wrote a life of Beethoven, which, however, is largely based on Schindler's.

At about the time I went to Leipsic the attitude of Moscheles toward Chopin was very like what Dionysius Weber's had

been toward Beethoven.   One of the
daughters of Moscheles was very fond of
playing Chopin, but her father forbade it.
Afterward she married and went to London, where she played Chopin to her
heart's content.   It is curious how men
who in their younger days are pioneers
become so conservative as they grow older
that they are like stone walls in the paths
of progress.   They forget that in their
youth they laughed at or criticized their
elders for the same pedantry of which
they themselves afterward become guilty.

### THE INTIMACY OF MOSCHELES AND MENDELSSOHN

MOSCHELES and Mendelssohn had been
warm friends.   Moscheles, in particular,
prided himself on the composer's friendship.   No one to-day can understand the
influence which Mendelssohn had upon
his contemporaries, by whom his music
and his personality were fairly worshiped.
Comparisons were made between him and
Beethoven to the latter's disadvantage.
I remember an excellent musician saying

to me, "Beethoven does have consecutive fifths now and then, Mendelssohn never." He did not realize that these apparent violations of technical rules were part of Beethoven's rugged strength, while Mendelssohn's scrupulous adherence to them was evidence of weakness.

Mendelssohn's death was a great shock to Moscheles. Mendelssohn had often visited him, and there was such profound musical sympathy between them that they were able to improvise together on two pianos. They understood each other so well that one of them would improvise a theme, which the other would follow. After a while they would interchange their rôles, the second piano taking up the theme, the first piano subordinating itself. This is not in itself an extraordinary feat, but it illustrates the musical sympathy which existed between Mendelssohn and Moscheles.

### SCHUMANN

FOR some years prior to 1844 Schumann lived in Leipsic. It was his habit to

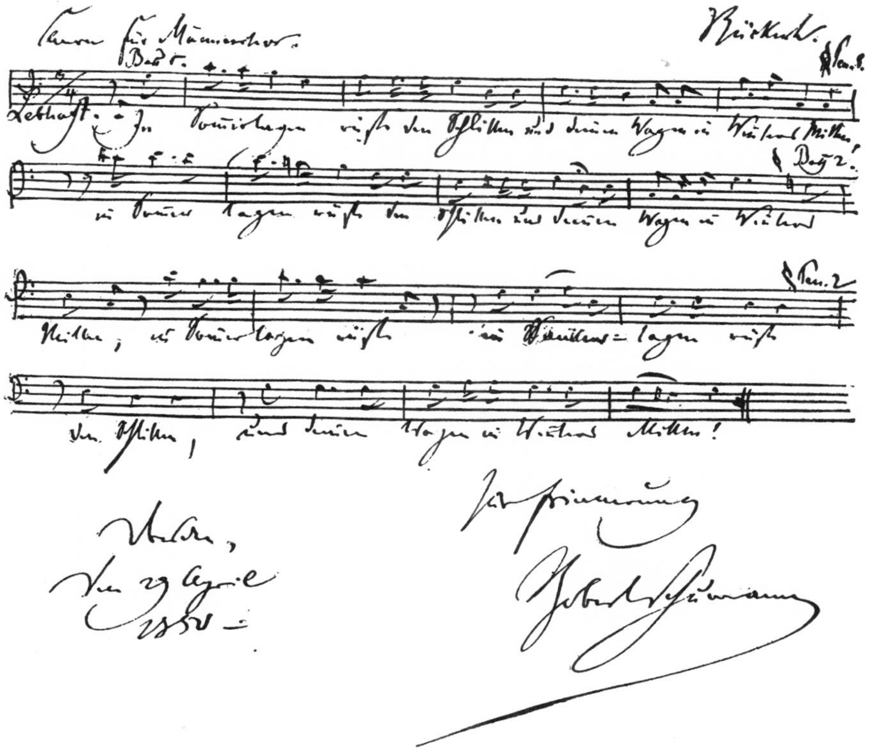
Canon für Männerchor.
Rückert.
Lebhaft.
Robert Schumann

compose intensely all day, and then to walk to a beer-cellar at the upper end of the Grimmaische Strasse. There he would sit at a table with one of his most trusted friends, an odd-looking but able musician and piano-teacher named Wenzel. There were two or three other musicians who frequented the place and were generally at the same table. Schumann enjoyed being among friends, but disliked nothing more than the restraint of social functions. No doubt there was a large consumption of beer, after the fashion of the Germans on such occasions, but to a musical student who could sit within hearing there was afforded a golden opportunity of absorbing musical ideas.

### SCHUMANN'S "SYMPHONY NO. 1, B FLAT"

WHEN I went to Germany, Schumann was living in Dresden, but he made frequent visits to Leipsic. I knew little or nothing of Schumann's music, for Mendelssohn then dominated the musical world; but the first orchestral composition of Schumann's that I ever heard placed him far above Mendelssohn in my estimation. It was at the second concert I attended at the Gewandhaus in Leipsic, and the work was the "First Symphony." I was so wrought up by it that I hummed passages from it as I walked home, and sat down at the piano when I got there, and played as much of it as I could remember. I hardly slept that night for the excitement of it. The first thing I did in the morning was to go to Breitkopf & Härtel's and buy the score, the orchestral parts and piano arrangements for four and two hands, and in these I fairly reveled.

I grew so enthusiastic over the symphony that I sent the score and parts to the Musical Fund Society of Boston, the only concert orchestra then in that city, and conducted by Mr. Webb. They could make nothing of the symphony, and it lay on the shelf for one or two years. Then they tried it again, saw something in it, but somehow could not get the swing of it, possibly on account of the syncopations.

Before my return from Europe in 1854, I think they finally played it.   In speaking of it, Mr. Webb said to my father : "Yes, it is interesting ; but in our next concert we play Haydn's 'Surprise Symphony,' and that will live long after this symphony of Schumann's is forgotten."   Many years afterward I reminded Mr. Webb of this remark, whereupon he said, "William, is it possible that I was so foolish ? "

Only a few years before I arrived at Leipsic, Schumann's genius was so little appreciated that when he entered the store of Breitkopf & Härtel with a new manuscript under his arm, the clerks would nudge one another and laugh.   One of them told me that they regarded him as a crank and a failure because his pieces remained on the shelf and were in the way.

I often saw Schumann in Leipsic, and I heard him conduct his cantata, "The Pilgrimage of the Rose."   His conducting was awkward, as he was neither active nor of commanding presence.   However, I liked his looks, as he seemed good-na-

tured, though perhaps not like a man
with whom one might easily become acquainted. This impression, however, may
be due to anecdotes which I had heard
regarding his lack of sociability.

### SCHUMANN'S ABSENT-MINDEDNESS

UP to the time of Mendelssohn's death his
followers and the small body of musicians
who appreciated Schumann had rubbed
pretty hard together. Naturally, Moscheles and Schumann had not been intimate. But Moscheles felt Mendelssohn's
loss so keenly that he cast about for some
one to take his place, and finally decided
to make overtures to Schumann by in-
viting him to his house to supper. What
occurred there was told to me by a fellow-
pupil. He said that while the company
was gathering in the drawing-room, Schumann sat in a corner apparently absorbed
in thought, without looking at any one or
uttering a word. He did not impress my
friend as morose, but rather as a man
whose thoughts were at the moment in an
entirely different sphere. Supper was

announced, and the guests being seated, it was discovered that there was a vacant place at the table. Moscheles looked about for Schumann, but he was not there. The host and several guests went back to the salon to look for him, and found him sitting in his corner, still deep in thought. When aroused, he said, "Oh, I had n't noticed that you had gone out." Then he went in to supper, but hardly said a word. What a contrast there was between his personality and that of the ever-affable, polished Mendelssohn! There is the same contrast between their music : Schumann's profound, and appealing to us most when we wish to withdraw entirely within the very sanctuary of our own emotions; Mendelssohn's smooth, finished, and easily understood.

Early in 1844 Schumann had moved to Dresden, and I called upon him in that city and received a pleasant welcome, contrary to my expectation, for I had heard much of his reticence. Judging by the brief entry in my diary, nothing of importance was said. I could not see Mme. Schumann, because she was giving

a lesson.   This was on April 13, 1850.   I
called again later in the month, and Schumann gave me his musical autograph, a
canon for male voices; and the next day
I received an autograph from Clara Schumann.   In 1880 I learned from Mme.
Schumann that the canon referred to had
already been published at the time when
I received it from Schumann.   (See Op.
65, No. 6.)

Afterward, when I met Wagner I could
not help contrasting his lively manner
and glowing enthusiasm with Schumann's
reserve, which, however, was by no means
repellent.   Indeed, if I had been the
greatest living musician, instead of a
mere boy student, Wagner could not
have received me with more kindness,
or have talked to me more delightfully
during the three memorable hours of my
life which were spent with him.


MORITZ HAUPTMANN

MY teacher in harmony and counterpoint
was Moritz Hauptmann, a pupil of Spohr,

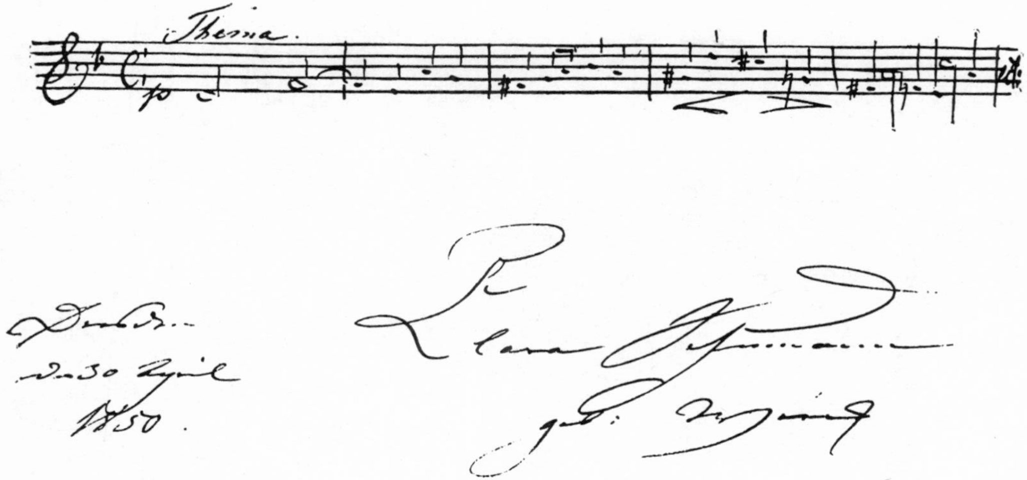
Thema.
Dresden den 30 April 1850.
Clara Schumann
geb: Wieck

and an excellent composer of church
music, his motets being especially beautiful.   He was the cantor and music director of the Thomas-schule at Leipsic, a
position which years before had been
held by Sebastian Bach.   He was altogether a genial and attractive man, of
gentle manner and disposition, and I at
once became much attached to him.   He
was in delicate health and suffered constantly from dyspepsia, yet bore all of his
ills with patience and equanimity.   I remember that he had a passion for baked
apples, one of the few things he could eat
without ill results, and on his stove, a
regular old-fashioned German structure
of porcelain, nearly as high as the ceiling,
there was always a row of apples in process of slow baking.

His autograph is one of the most curious in my book, and is an excellent example of his technical knowledge.   It is
a *Spiegel-Canon* ("looking-glass canon").
When held up to the mirror the reflection shows the answer to the canon in the
related key.

Not long after beginning my studies
under Hauptmann, I received from my
father a copy of his latest publication,
being a collection of tunes, mostly of his
own composition, for choir and congregational use in the church. He requested
me to show this to Hauptmann and get his
opinion, if practicable. I felt a decided
reluctance to do this, because I thought
my father's work was not worthy of the
notice of such a profound musician, so I
delayed the carrying out of his request.
After a few weeks, however, I began receiving letters from my father upon the
subject, and realized that I could not post-
pone action any longer. So one day, going
to my lesson, I took the book with me.
I kept it as well out of sight as I could
during the lesson, and then at the last
moment, when about to leave the room,
I placed it on Hauptmann's table, telling
him in an apologetic way of my father's
request and seeking to excuse myself for
troubling him. I said I was afraid he
would find nothing in the book to interest
him.

When the regular time for my lesson recurred I hesitated to present myself again; but there was no way of avoiding the difficulty, so with a tremendous exercise of will I faced the situation. What was my surprise and relief when he greeted me with "Mr. Mason, I have examined your father's book with much interest and pleasure, and his admirable treatment of the voices is most musicianly and satisfactory. Please give him my sincere regards, and thank him for his attention in sending me the book."

At the moment I could not understand how such a big contrapuntist could express himself in such strong terms of approval; but I knew him to be genuine, and so I straightened myself up and really began to be proud of my father. Another and more important result was the recognition of my own ignorance in imagining that a thing in order to be great must necessarily be intricate and complicated. It dawned upon me that the simplest things are sometimes the grandest and the most difficult of attainment.

I also took lessons in instrumentation from Ernst Friedrich Richter, a pupil of Hauptmann.

### A VISIT TO WAGNER.

MY parents joined me in Leipsic in January, 1852, and in the spring of that year we planned a tour which was to take us to Switzerland in June.

In Leipsic I made the acquaintance of a man named Albert Wagner, meeting him quite frequently at the restaurant where I took my meals. While I was planning the tour, I chanced to mention it to him, and when he heard that I was going to Zürich, he said : "My brother, Richard Wagner, lives there. I will give you a letter of introduction to him." This was the first intimation I had that Albert was a brother of the composer. I suppose he had not thought it worth while to tell me. Richard was still under a political cloud in Saxony, and was compelled to live in exile on account of the part he had taken in the revolution

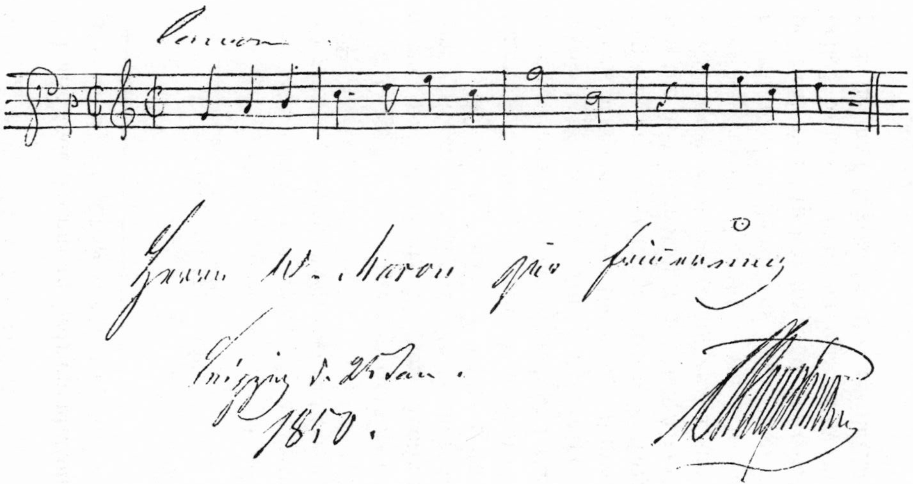
Canon
1850.

of 1848; nor was his reputation as a composer then so general that Albert would have thought his kinship much to boast of.

We reached Zürich on June 5, 1852, and, the next morning, armed with the letter, I made my way to Wagner's chalet, which was situated on a hill in the suburbs. It was then about ten o'clock in the morning.

When I asked the maid who opened the door if Herr Wagner was at home and to be seen, she answered, as I had feared she would, that he was busily at work in his study, and could not be disturbed. I handed her my letter of introduction, and asked her to give it to Herr Wagner, and to say to him that I was expecting to remain in Zürich three or four days, and would call again, hoping to be fortunate enough to find him disengaged.

Just as I was turning to leave, I heard a voice at the head of the stairs call out, "Wer ist da?" I told the maid to deliver my letter immediately. As soon as Wagner had glanced through it, he exclaimed,

"Kommen Sie herauf! Kommen Sie herauf!"

At that time Wagner was known, and that not widely, only as the composer of "Rienzi," "The Flying Dutchman," "Tannhäuser," and "Lohengrin." I had heard only "The Flying Dutchman," but considered it a most beautiful work, and was eager to meet the composer.

Wagner's first words, as I met him on the landing at the head of the stairs, were: "You 've come just at the right time. I 've been working away at something, and I 'm stuck. I 'm in a state of nervous irritation, and it is absolutely impossible for me to go on. So I 'm glad you 've come."

I remember perfectly my first impression of him. He looked to me much more like an American than a German. After asking about his brother, he began questioning me in a lively way about his friends in Leipsic, about the concerts and opera there, and the works that had been given. He also asked most kindly after my own affairs—what I was doing, with whom I had studied, how long

I intended to remain, what my plans were
for the future, and most particularly about
musical matters in America.   In some way
Beethoven was mentioned.   After that the
conversation became a monologue with me
as a listener, for Wagner began to talk so
fluently and enthusiastically about Beethoven that I was quite content to keep si-
lent and to avoid interrupting his eloquent
oration.

### WAGNER ON MENDELSSOHN
### AND BEETHOVEN

As he warmed up to the subject, he began
to draw comparisons between Beethoven
and Mendelssohn.   "Mendelssohn," he
said, "was a gentleman of refinement and
high degree; a man of culture and polished
manner; a courtier who was always at
home in evening dress.   As was the man,
so is his music, full of elegance, grace,
finish, and refinement, but carried without variance to such a degree that at times
one longs for brawn and muscle.   Yet it
is music that is always exquisite, fairy-
like, and fine in character.   In Beethoven
we get the man of brawn and muscle.   He

was too inspired to pay much attention to conventionalities. He went right to the pith of what he had to say, and said it in a robust, decisive, manly, yet tender way, brushing aside the methods and amenities of conventionalism, and striking at once at the substance of what he wished to express. Notwithstanding its robustness, his music is at times inexpressibly tender; but it is a manly tenderness, and carries with it an idea of underlying and sustaining strength. Some years ago, when I was kapellmeister in Dresden, I had a remarkable experience, which illustrates the invigorating and refreshing power of Beethoven's music. It was at one of the series of afternoon concerts of classic music given at the theater. The day was hot and muggy, and everybody seemed to be in a state of lassitude and incapacity for mental or physical effort. On glancing at the program, I noticed that by some chance all of the pieces I had selected were in the minor mode—first, Mendelssohn's exquisite 'A Minor Symphony,' music in dress-suit and white kid

gloves, spotless and *comme il faut* ; then an
overture by Cherubini ; and finally Beethoven's 'Symphony No. 5, in C Minor.' "
At this point Wagner rose from his chair,
and began walking about the room.
"Everybody," he continued, "was listless
and languid, and the atmosphere seemed
damp and spiritless. The orchestra labored wearily through the symphony and
overture, while the audience became more
and more apathetic. It seemed impossible to arouse either players or listeners,
and I thought seriously of dismissing both
after the overture. I was very reluctant
to subject Beethoven's wonderfully beautiful music to such a crucial test, but after
a moment's reflection I appreciated the
fact that here was an opportunity for
proving the strength and virility of it,
and I said to myself, 'I will have courage,
and stick to my program.' "

Wagner stopped walking a moment, and
looked about the room as if searching for
something. Then he rushed to a corner,
and seizing a walking-stick, raised it as if
it were a baton.

"Here is Beethoven," he exclaimed, "the working-man in his shirt-sleeves, with his great herculean breast bared to the elements."

He straightened himself up, and, giving the stick a swing, brought it down with an abrupt "Ta-ta-ta-tum !"—the opening measure of Beethoven's "C Minor Symphony" :

The whole scene was graphically portrayed. Then throwing himself into a chair, he said : "The effect was electrical on orchestra and audience. There was no more apathy. The air was cleared as by a passing thunder-shower. There was the test."

When Wagner spoke of Mendelssohn, his tone of voice indicated the gentle refinement of the courtier and his music. When he mentioned Beethoven, his manner was animated and full of enthusiasm.

Wagner's enthusiasm, his openness in taking me at once into his musical confi-

dence, fascinated me, and gave me an
insight into the wonderful vitality and
energy of the man. He was planning a
tramp through the Tyrol, about a week
later, with a professor from the Zürich
University. "Come along with us," he
said. "Alle guten Dinge sind drei" ("All
good things are three"). However, I did
not feel at liberty to leave my parents to
continue their trip alone, as I was acting
as interpreter for them. Of course Wagner was not then what he afterward became in the eyes of the world. I now
know what I missed.

A WAGNER AUTOGRAPH

BUT I did not leave Wagner's house without what many musicians, to whom I have
shown it, consider one of the most interesting musical autographs ever penned.
It is autographic from beginning to end,
even to the lines of the staff; for when I
asked Wagner for his autograph, he drew
them himself on a sheet of blank paper,
and then wrote what is evidently the germ

of the dragon motive in "The Ring of the Nibelung." It is dated June 5, 1852, and it is particularly interesting that he should have written this motive at that time. From his correspondence with Liszt, it is clear that he had not yet finished the poem of the "Walküre," and had not yet begun the score of the cycle. He wrote the books of the "Ring" backward, but in the composition of the cycle he began with the "Rheingold," in the autumn of the year in which I met him. The dragon motive occurs in the "Rheingold," but in quite a different form. He .began the "Walküre" in June, 1854, two years later, completing it in 1856. In the meantime, in the autumn of 1854, he also began the music of "Siegfried," and it is in the first act of this music drama, written more than two years after I had met him, that we find the dragon motive exactly as it is written in my autograph, except that it is transposed a tone lower, and that the length of the notes is changed, though their relative value is the same, dotted halves being substituted for quarters.

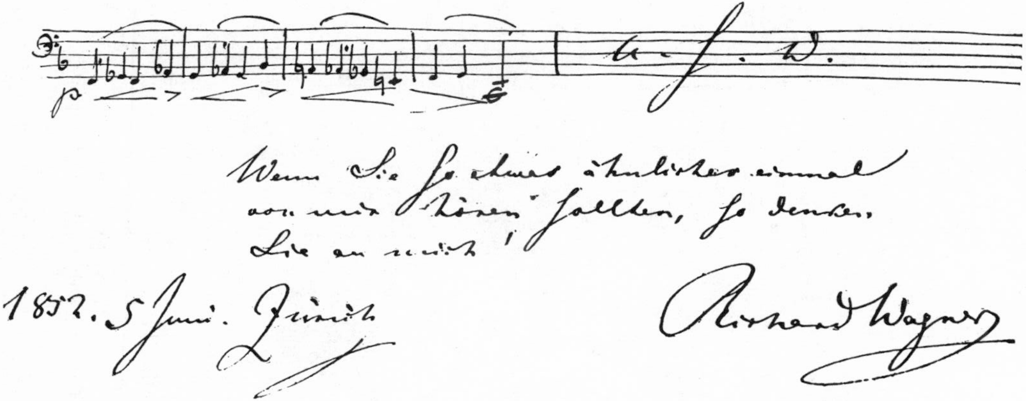
p
a. f. W.
Wenn Sie so etwas ähnliches einmal
von mir hören sollten, so denken
Sie an mich!
1852. 5 Juni. Zürich
Richard Wagner

The passage will be found on page 7 of Klindworth's piano-score of "Siegfried." This, I believe, is the only place in the four divisions of the "Ring" where the motive appears in this form.

Added significance and value are given to the autograph by the lines which Wagner wrote under it, and which are signed and dated : "Wenn Sie so etwas ähnliches einmal von mir hören sollten, so denken Sie an mich !" ("If you ever hear anything of mine like this, then think of me.") Even this was characteristic of the man. "Siegfried" was not heard until nearly a quarter of a century after he had written a passage from it in my autograph-book—*but it was heard.*

### MOSCHELES

The playing of Moscheles was in a direct line of descent from Clementi and Hummel, and just preceded the Thalberg school. Moscheles was fond of quoting these authorities and of holding them up as excellent examples for his pupils. He advocated a very quiet hand position, confining, as far as possible, whatever motion was necessary to finger and hand muscles; and by way of illustration he said that Clementi's hands were so level in position and quiet in motion that he could easily keep a crown-piece on the back of his hand while playing the most rapid scale passages.

I was not much surprised at this, for I knew it had been said of Henry C. Timm of New York, an admirable pianist of the Hummel school, that he could play a scale with a glass of wine on the back of his hand without spilling a drop. I, boy-like, could not resist the temptation to repeat what I had heard. There was a curious expression upon the face of our good teacher, which gave the impression that he thought it a pretty tall story, and my fellow-pupils put it down as a yarn prompted by desire on my part to get ahead of Moscheles. Among these was Charles Wehle of Prague, of whom I saw a good deal. Some years later, after I had left Weimar for America, Wehle happened to visit Liszt. My name was mentioned, and Wehle asked, "Did you ever hear his wonderful tale about Timm, the New York player?" Then he repeated the anecdote, but changed the glass of wine to a glass of water. Liszt shook his head incredulously, and said, "Mason never said anything about a glass of water all the time he was in Weimar."

Moscheles was an excellent pianist and teacher, but he was already growing old, and his playing of sforzando and strongly accented tones was apt to be accompanied by an audible snort, which was far from musical. However, as a Bach-player he was especially great, and it was a delight to hear him. One evening, after my lesson, he began playing the preludes and fugues from the "Well-tempered Clavier," and I was enchanted with the finish, repose, and musicianship of his performance, which was without fuss or show. I have never heard any one surpass him in Bach.

Paderewski's Bach-playing is much like

that of my old teacher.   Several years
ago, in company with Adolf Brodsky, the
violinist, I attended one of Paderewski's
recitals given in this city.   After listening
to compositions of Bach and Beethoven,
Brodsky said : "He lays everything from
A to Z before you in the most conscientious way, and through delicacy and sensitiveness of perception he attains a very
close and artistic adjustment of values."

Thoroughly in accord with Brodsky, I
vividly recall the similarity of Paderewski's interpretation to that of Moscheles,
both being characterized by perfect repose in action, while at the same time not
lacking in intensity of expression.   The
modern adaptations and alterations from
Bach are not here referred to, but the
music as originally written by the composer.   In Paderewski's conception and
performance, like that of Moscheles, each
and all of the voices received careful and
reverent attention, and were brought out
with due regard to their relative, as well
as to their individual, importance.   Nuances were never neglected, neither were

they in excess. Thus the musical requirements of polyphonic interpretation were
artistically fulfilled. Head and heart
were united in skilful combination and
loving response.

While I was in Leipsic, Moscheles celebrated his silver wedding, and one of the
features of the occasion was odd and interesting. I forget whether I had the
story direct from him or from one of my
fellow-students. It is as follows : At the
time Moscheles was paying attention to
the lady who afterward became his wife
he had a rival who was a farmer. What
became of the farmer after Moscheles carried off the prize history does not make
clear. A friend of Moscheles, an artist of
ability, conceived the unique idea of com-
memorating the joyous anniversary, and,
putting it into act, he painted two portraits of Mrs. Moscheles, one representing
her as she appeared on that interesting
occasion, and the other giving his idea of
how she would have looked after twenty-
five years of wedded life had she married
the farmer.

JOSEPH JOACHIM

"LEIPSIC, Wednesday, September 19, 1849." Under this date I find in my diary a note to the effect that Joachim the violinist made me a friendly call at half-past ten o'clock. I had previously called on him to present a letter of introduction which I had received in Hamburg from Mortier de Fontaine.

Joachim made a marked impression upon me as being genial and unassuming in manner. He very cordially invited me to come to his room, saying, "We will play sonatas for violin and pianoforte together." This afforded a fine opportunity to a young piano-student, and, coming as it did without solicitation or expectation, was all the more appreciated. Less than two weeks later, on September 30, I heard him play the Mendelssohn violin concerto at the first Gewandhaus concert of the season, and was enchanted with his musical interpretation of the beautiful composition. A little further on in the diary it is written that the second Gewandhaus

concert was given on October 7. The
Schumann "Symphony in B Flat Major,
No. 1," was played, and "I never before
experienced such a thrill of enthusiasm."
On Thursday, October 18, the third Gewandhaus concert took place, the symphony being by Spohr, "No. 3, C Minor."
An item of special interest regarding this
concert is that I heard here for the first
time the fine violoncellist Bernhard Cossmann, with whom, in later years, I became
intimately acquainted. He was then in
the Weimar orchestra and the Ferdinand
Laub String Quartet, and was one of our
"Weimarische Dutzbrüder."

### SCHUMANN'S "CONCERTO IN A MINOR"

THIS concerto I heard for the first time
in Leipsic, on Saturday, January 19, 1850.
It was in one of the Euterpe Society's concerts, exceedingly well played by Adolph
Blassman of Dresden, and I vividly remember the stunning effect it produced
upon some of the best pupils of the Conservatory who were present. I was nearly

as much excited over the composition as I had previously been at the performance of the "Symphony in B Flat Major."

A few weeks later the same concerto was played in a Gewandhaus concert by Fräulein Wilhelmine Clauss, a pupil of Mme. Schumann, who had studied it under her supervision. The result was another good rendering, although at the previous rehearsal there had been trouble with the so-called syncopated passage where the $\frac{3}{2}$ and $\frac{3}{4}$ rhythms alternate, and it was not until after many repeated attempts that success was attained.

On account of the long, uninterrupted continuance of this $\frac{3}{2}$ rhythm its character as a syncopation is entirely lost and it becomes simply an augmentation of the preceding and following $\frac{3}{2}$ rhythm, and all of the best orchestral conductors I have seen always give out the beat accordingly—that is, in a manner equivalent to simply doubling the rate of speed in the $\frac{3}{4}$ from that of the $\frac{3}{2}$ movement. I do not see how the performers, both in orchestra and piano, can be kept together in any other way.

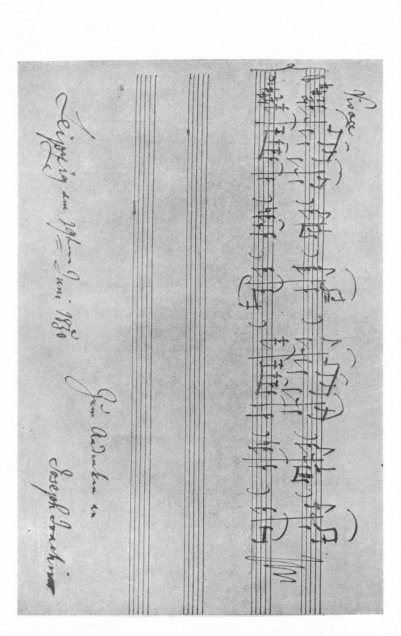

## CARL MAYER

FROM Leipsic I went to Dresden in March, 1850, and stayed there a few months with some American friends who were studying the pianoforte under Carl Mayer, whose very beautiful and finished playing was more adapted for the salon than for the concert-hall. Although I took no lessons of him, I constantly enjoyed his society, frequently heard him play, and in this way profited much from the association.

I wished, however, to get to work in the more advanced and modern methods, and so decided to go to Alexander Drey-schock in Prague. My departure from Dresden was somewhat delayed because, upon going to the Austrian consul's to get his visé, he refused to give it to me. This was owing to the political disturbances which had taken place in Europe a year or two before. Thereupon I wrote to Dreyschock for his assistance, and being on friendly terms with the Austrian minister at Dresden, he easily accomplished the desired result.

### DREYSCHOCK

ALEXANDER DREYSCHOCK was one of the most distinguished pianoforte-virtuosos of his time, and his specialty was his wonderful octave-playing. Indeed, he acquired such fame in this particular that the mention of "octave-playing" at once suggested the name of Dreyschock to his contemporaries. He was also celebrated on account of his highly trained left hand, so much so that Saphir, the famous Vienna critic, paid tribute to the fact by writing a stanza which obtained wide circulation, and which runs as follows:

> Welchen Titel der nicht hinke
> Man dem Meister geben möchte,
> Der zur Rechten macht die Linke? —
> Nennt ihn, "Doctor beider Rechte."

An anecdote, related to me by one of his most intimate friends not long after my arrival in Prague, is interesting in this connection, as well as instructive to piano-students. Tomaschek, his teacher, was in the habit of receiving a few friends on stated occasions for the purpose of musical entertainment and conversation. One evening the rapid progress in piano-technic was being discussed, and Tomaschek remarked that more and more in this direction was demanded each day. A copy of Chopin's "Études, Op. 10," open at "Étude No. 12, C Minor," happened to be lying on the piano-desk. It will be remembered that the left-hand part of this étude consists throughout of rapid passages in single notes, difficult enough in the original to satisfy the ambition of most pianists. Tomaschek, looking at this, remarked, "I should not wonder if, one of these days, a pianist should appear who would play all of these single-note left-hand passages in octaves." Dreyschock, overhearing the remark, at once conceived an idea which he proceeded next day to carry into execution. For a period of six successive weeks, at the rate of twelve hours a day, he practised the étude in accordance with the suggestion of Tomaschek. How he ever survived the effort is a mystery, but, at any rate, when the next musical evening at Tomaschek's occurred he was present, and, watching his opportunity for a favorable moment, sat down to the pianoforte and played the étude in a brilliant and triumphant manner, with the left-hand octaves, thus fulfilling the prediction of Tomaschek. Upon a subsequent occasion he repeated this feat at one of the Leipsic Gewandhaus concerts. Mendelssohn, as I am told, was present, and was very demonstrative in the expression of his delight and astonishment. I will add, for the benefit of those of my readers, should there be any, who are inclined to try the experiment, that certain adaptations are necessary in various parts of the étude in order to get the required scope for the left-hand octaves. Thus, the opening octave passage in the beginning must be played an octave higher than it was originally written.

At the time of which I write (1849–50) very little seems to have been known of the important influence of the upper-arm muscles and their very efficient agency, when properly employed, in the production of tone-quality and volume by means of increased relaxation, elasticity, and springiness in their movements.

I received considerably over one hundred lessons from Dreyschock, and with slow and rapid scale and arpeggio practice his instruction had special reference to limber and flexible wrists, his distinguishing feature being his wonderful octave-playing. Beyond the wrists, however, the other arm muscles received practically little or no attention, and the fact is that during my whole stay abroad none of my teachers or their pupils, with many of whom I was intimately associated, seemed to know anything about the importance of the upper-arm muscles, the practical knowledge of which I had acquired through the playing of Leopold de Meyer as described in the earlier part of this book. In the Tomaschek method, as taught and practised by Dreyschock, the direction to the pupil was simply to keep the wrists loose. To be sure, this could not be altogether accomplished without some degree of arm-limberness, but no specific directions were given for cultivating the latter. So far as wrist-motion is concerned, Leschetitsky's manner of playing octaves has much in common with the Tomaschek-Dreyschock method, if the former may be judged from the playing of most of his pupils, who seem to pay but little attention to the upper-arm muscles. This is quite natural when it is remembered that Leschetitsky was in some sense an assistant of Dreyschock when the latter was at the head of the piano department in the Conservatory of Music at St. Petersburg. The Leschetitsky pupils, however, have a manner of sinking the wrists below the keyboard which was not in accordance with Dreyschock's manner of playing. It seems to me that the latter's method of level wrists is more productive of a full, sonorous, musical tone.

I remained with Dreyschock for over a year, taking three lessons a week and practising about five hours a day. I played also in private musicales at the houses of the nobility and at the homes of

some of the wealthy Jews, two classes of
society which were entirely distinct from
each other, never mingling in private life.
I met and became well acquainted with
Jules Schulhoff, whose compositions for
the pianoforte were very effective, but
more appropriate to the drawing-room
than to the concert-hall.

### PRINCE DE ROHAN'S DINNER

IT was customary in Prague to give once
a year an orchestral concert of high order,
the pecuniary proceeds of which were for
the benefit of the poor, and on one of
these occasions I played with orchestra a
brilliant composition of Dreyschock's entitled "Salut à Vienne."   It was also the
custom, in concerts of this order, to use
the name of some nobleman—the higher
the better—as patron.   On this occasion
the name used was that of the Prince de
Rohan, a French nobleman who, expatri-
ated, had lived for some time in Prague
in a palace of the old Austrian Emperor
Ferdinand, who, shortly before the time

of which I write, had abdicated in favor of his nephew, the present emperor. A few days after the concert, while I was practising in my modestly appointed room, there was a loud knock at the door, and immediately there entered a servant of the prince in gorgeous livery, who, advancing to the middle of the room and straightening himself up, announced in stentorian tones, "His Highness Prince Rohan invites you to dinner," at the same time handing me a large envelop with a big seal on the back. Without waiting for a reply, he made a low obeisance and left the room.

It turned out that all the principal artists who had taken part in the concert had been invited to the dinner, and on the appointed day one of these, an opera-singer of distinction, came to my room and asked if he might go with me. Never having been to a prince's house, and not knowing what ceremony might be considered appropriate to such an occasion, he conceived the idea of securing a chaperon. The incongruity of his selecting

a green American youth for this purpose
greatly amused me, but I said, "Come
along; they won't hang us for anything
we are likely to do." Arriving at the
palace five or ten minutes before the hour,
the porter at the outer gate refused us
admission, saying we were too early.
This untoward reception somewhat un-
settled us for the moment, but there was
nothing for us to do but to walk about
until the appointed time. On presenting
ourselves again at the gate at precisely
the right moment, we were promptly
admitted. After passing through the
hands of several servants, we were finally
ushered into the presence of the prince.

He was not an imposing man in appearance, neither was he as well dressed as
several of the four or five guests who arrived later, my companion and I being
the first-comers. The prince offered me
his arm, and led me through the picture-
gallery adjoining the reception-room,
pointing out the portraits of his ancestors,
whose names were mostly familiar to me
from French history. As all formality in

his manner had passed away, I found the occasion intensely interesting.

Dinner being announced, we proceeded to the dining-room, and, when we were seated, the prince said that he would greet us first with a glass of Schloss Johannisberger Cabìnet wine, which he had just received from his friend Prince Metternich, the owner of that world-renowned vineyard. As is well known, this Cabinet wine is never on the market, and can be bought only at an administrator's sale, and then commands the highest price. It is not unusual for tourists to pay a large price for this wine on the spot, even then not getting the genuine thing, for the space where the Cabinet wine grows is very small compared with the quantity of wine which is credited to it. Several kinds of red and white wines were served, and various kinds of German beer, as well as English and Scotch ale. Finally, after seven or eight courses, a single glass of champagne—no more—was poured out for each guest. Liquid refreshments, however, did not end there, for we after-

ward adjourned to the library, where we
found a roaring wood fire in a vast stone
chimney-place, where cigars, liqueurs of
many kinds, and finally coffee and tea
with rum were served.     There was no
music.

### CHOPIN, HENSELT, AND THALBERG

I HAD always looked forward to taking
lessons of Chopin at some period during
my sojourn in Europe, but this was not
accomplished, on account of his death,
which took place in Paris on October 17,
1849.     Neither did I ever hear him play.
One of Dreyschock's anecdotes about him
is interesting as well as instructive, for it
conveys an idea of one of the principal
characteristics of his style.     Dreyschock
told me that, a few years before, Chopin
gave a recital of his own compositions in
Paris, which he, Dreyschock, attended in
company with Thalberg.     They listened
with delight throughout the performance,
but on reaching the street Thalberg began
shouting at the top of his voice.

"What 's the matter?" asked Dreyschock, in astonishment.

"Oh," said Thalberg, "I 've been listening to *piano* all the evening, and now, for
the sake of contrast, I want a little *forte*."

Dreyschock spoke of Chopin's extremely delicate and exquisite playing,
but said that he lacked the physical
strength to produce forte effects by contrast in accordance with his own ideas.
This is illustrated by another anecdote
which I heard many years afterward from
Korbay.   A young and robust pianist had
been playing Chopin's "Polonaise Mili-
taire" to the composer, and had broken
a string.   When, in confusion, he began
to apologize, Chopin said to him, "Young
man, if I had your strength and played
that polonaise as it should be played,
there would n't be a sound string left in
the instrument by the time I got through."

The distinguishing characteristic of
Chopin's piano-playing was his lovely
musical and poetic tone, his warm and
emotional coloring, and his impassioned
utterance.   In those days one was not afraid

to play with a great deal of sentiment,
although pianists who were capable of
doing this poetically were rare. In modern
times it has become the fashion to ridicule
any tendency toward emotional playing
and to extol the intellectual side beyond
its just proportion.   It seems to me that
there should be a happy combination and
a delicate and well-proportioned adjustment between the temperamental and intellectual, with a slight preponderance of
the former.

An anecdote of Adolf Henselt, also related to me by Dreyschock, is entertaining
as well as suggestive, especially to pianoforte-players, who are constantly troubled
with nervousness when playing before an
audience.   Henselt, whose home was in
St. Petersburg, was in the habit of spend-
ing a few weeks every summer with a
relative who lived in Dresden.   Dreyschock, passing through that city, called
on him one morning, and upon going up
the staircase to his room, heard the most
lovely tones of the pianoforte imaginable.

He was so fascinated that he sat down

at the top of the landing and listened for
a long time.  Henselt was playing re-
peatedly the same composition, and his
playing was also specially characterized
by a warm emotional touch and a deli-
cious legato, causing the tones to melt, as
it were, one into the other, and this, too,
without any confusion or lack of clearness.
Henselt was full of sentiment, but detested "sentimentality."  Finally, for lack
of time, Dreyschock was obliged to an-
nounce himself, although, as he said, he
could have listened for hours.  He entered
the room, and after the usual friendly
greeting said, "What were you playing
just now as I came up the stairs?"  Henselt replied that he was composing a piece
and was playing it over to himself.  Dreyschock expressed his admiration of the
composition, and begged Henselt to play
it again.  Henselt, after prolonged urging,
sat down to the pianoforte and began playing again, but, alas! his performance was
stiff, inaccurate, and even clumsy, and all
of the exquisite poetry and unconscious-
ness of his style completely disappeared.

Dreyschock said that it was quite impossible to describe the difference ; and this was simply the result of diffidence and nervousness, which, as it appeared, were entirely out of the player's power to control. Pianoforte-players frequently experience this state of things. The only remedy is freedom from self-consciousness, which can best be achieved by earnest and persistent mental concentration.

### ANTON SCHINDLER, "AMI DE BEETHOVEN "

AFTER finishing my studies with Dreyschock, I went to Frankfort, not to study under any particular master, but in order to enjoy the opera and the musical life there. Moreover, two or three of my old Boston friends were temporarily settled there, pursuing their musical studies.

Anton Schindler, one of the well-known musical characters of the day, and who had been Beethoven's most intimate friend during the latter years of the great composer's life, lived at Frankfort, and,

being members of the same club, the Bürger Verein, I often enjoyed the pleasure
of his society, and heard much concerning
Beethoven. Schindler had written a life
of Beethoven, and was naturally very
proud of his close association with the
great master. During his residence in
Paris, some years previous to the time of
which I am writing, he caused to be
printed on his visiting-cards, "Anton
Schindler, Ami de Beethoven."

He worshiped his idol's memory, and
was so familiar with his music that the
slightest mistake in interpretation or departure from Beethoven's invention or
design jarred upon his nerves—or possibly
he made a pretense of this. He held all
four-hand pianoforte arrangements of
works designed and composed for orchestra as abominations. Extreme sensitiveness is a rôle sometimes assumed by men
in no wise remarkable, in order to enhance
their own importance in the eyes of others.
Schindler's attitude as to the undesira-
bility of orchestral pianoforte arrangements will meet with the approval of

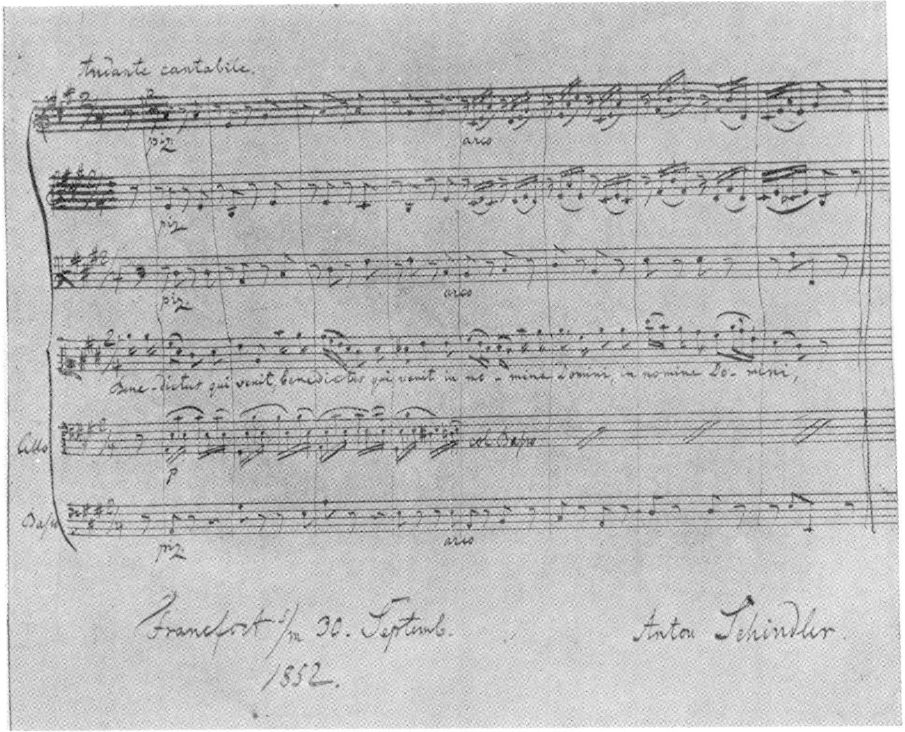
Andante cantabile.
pizz
arco
Bene-dictus qui venit, benedictus qui venit in no - mine Domini, in nomine Do - mini,
Cello
col Basso
p
Basso
Francfort a/m 30. Septemb.
1852.
Anton Schindler.

many, but he certainly carried his sensitiveness in regard to the interpretation of Beethoven's works to amusing extremes.

Every winter a subscription series of orchestral concerts was given in Frankfort, each program of which included at least one symphony. The concerts took place in a very old stone building called the "Museum," and on the occasion here referred to the symphony was Beethoven's "No. 5, C Minor." It so happened that, owing to long-continued rains and extreme humidity, the stone walls of the old hall were saturated with dampness, in fact, were actually wet. This excess of moisture affected the pitch of the wood wind-instruments to such a degree that the other instruments had to be adjusted to accommodate them. Schindler, it was noticed, left the hall at the close of the first movement. This seemed a strange proceeding on the part of the "Ami de Beethoven," and when later in the evening he was seen at the Bürger Verein and asked why he had gone away so suddenly, he replied gruffly, "I don't care to hear Beethoven's 'C Minor Symphony' played in the key of B minor."

## SCHINDLER AND SCHNYDER
### VON WARTENSEE

ANOTHER story current in Frankfort at this time further illustrates Schindler's peculiarity. Among the noted musicians living in Frankfort was a theoretician, Swiss by birth, named Schnyder von Wartensee, who was of considerable importance in his day. Schindler and Von Wartensee had lived in Frankfort, but had never met each other, although common friends had at various times made ineffectual efforts to bring them together. They were both advanced in years, and, as it seemed, ought to have been genial companions. Possibly the failure to arrange a meeting had been due to Wartensee's being older than Schindler, and thus in a position to expect the latter to call first, while Schindler, being "Ami de Beethoven," felt it beneath his dignity to make the first move. However, some time previous to my arrival another plan for an interview was contrived, and as so many previous ones had failed the outcome of this was watched with interest.

By the exercise of considerable diplomatic tact Schindler was persuaded to agree to call upon Wartensee and to fix a time for the visit. The friends of the gentlemen had all been looking forward with much interest to the result of this meeting, hoping thereby to hear a great many musical reminiscences, and a committee was appointed to watch Schindler and make sure that he kept the appointment. After a while the committee returned to the Bürger Verein and reported that they had seen him almost reach Wartensee's house, then pause for a moment, and suddenly turn and hurry away. Later Schindler himself came in, and being questioned concerning the interview, exclaimed, "Bah! as I got near the house I heard them [Wartensee and his wife] playing a four-handed piano arrangement of the 'Eroica.'"

### FIRST LONDON CONCERT

In January, 1853, my stay in Frankfort was brought to an end by a letter from Sir Julius Benedict, asking me to come to London to play at one of the concerts of the Harmonic Union at Exeter Hall. I accepted the engagement, and made my first appearance in London under Benedict's conductorship, playing Weber's "Concertstück." An account having been published in a London paper of the very delightful celebration, in 1899, of my seventieth birthday by my pupils, past and present, and by many of my friends, I received an inquiry from a lady living in London, asking whether I was the same William Mason whom she had heard in Exeter Hall nearly half a century ago !

I accepted only one other engagement to play in public, though I remained near London for more than two months, just to look about.

I was much impressed with the extent to which Mendelssohn's influence prevailed in English matters musical. I met a great many excellent musicians there, especially several fine organists; but a large majority, both in their ideas and in their style of playing and composition, were nothing but Mendelssohns in "half-tone," and to some extent this is still true of England.

## WITH LISZT IN WEIMAR

AFTER my London visit I was obliged to return to Leipsic to transact some business, and I decided to call on Liszt in Weimar en route. My intention was to make another effort to be received by him as a pupil, my idea being, if he declined, to go to Paris and study under some French master.

I reached Weimar on the 14th of April, 1853, and put up at the Hotel zum Erbprinzen. At that time Liszt occupied a house on the Altenburg belonging to the grand duke. The old grand duke, under whose patronage Goethe had made Weimar famous, was still living. I think his idea was to make Weimar as famous musically through Liszt as it had been in literature in Goethe's time.

Having secured my room at the Erbprinzen, I set out for the Altenburg. The butler who opened the door mistook me for a wine-merchant whom he had been expecting. I explained that I was not that person. "This is my card," I said. "I have come here from London to see Liszt." He took the card, and returned almost immediately with the request for me to enter the dining-room.

I found Liszt at the table with another man. They were drinking their after-dinner coffee and cognac. The moment Liszt saw me he exclaimed, "Nun, Mason, Sie lassen lange auf sich warten!" ("Well, Mason, you let people wait for you a long time!") I suppose he saw my surprised look, for he added, "Ich habe Sie schon vor vier Jahren erwartet" ("I have been expecting you for four years"). Then it struck me that I had probably wholly misinterpreted his first letter to me and what he said when I called on him during the Goethe festival. But nothing was said about my remaining, and though he was most affable, I began to doubt whether I would accomplish the object of my visit.

### ACCEPTED BY LISZT

WHEN we rose from the table and went into the drawing-room, Liszt said: "I have a new piano from Érard of Paris. Try it, and see how you like it." He asked me to pardon him if he moved about the room, for he had to get together some papers which it was necessary to take with him, as he was going to the palace of the grand duke. "As the palace is on the way to the hotel, we can walk as far as that together," he added.

I felt intuitively that my opportunity had come. I sat down at the piano with the idea that I would not endeavor to show Liszt how to play, but would play as simply as if I were alone. I played "Amitié pour Amitié," a little piece of my own which had just been published by Hofmeister of Leipsic.

"That's one of your own?" asked Liszt when I had finished. "Well, it's a charming little piece." Still nothing was said about my being accepted as a pupil. But when we left the Altenburg, he said casu-

LISZT IN MIDDLE LIFE

ally, "You say you are going to Leipsic
for a few days on business? While there
you had better select your piano and have
it sent here. Meanwhile I will tell Klindworth to look up rooms for you. Indeed,
there is a vacant room in the house in
which he lives, which is pleasantly situated
just outside the limits of the ducal park."

I can still recall the thrill of joy which
passed through me when Liszt spoke these
words. They left no doubt in my mind.
I was accepted as his pupil. We walked
down the hill toward the town, Liszt
leaving me when we arrived at the palace,
telling me, however, that he would call
later at the hotel and introduce me to
my fellow-pupils. About eight o'clock
that evening he came.

After smoking a cigar and chatting
with me for half an hour, Liszt proposed
going down to the café, saying, "The
gentlemen are probably there, as this is
about their regular hour for supper."
Proceeding to the dining-room, we found
Messrs. Raff, Pruckner, and Klindworth,
to whom I was presented in due form,

and who received me in a very friendly manner.

I had no idea then, neither have I now, what Liszt's means were, but I learned soon after my arrival at Weimar that he never took pay from his pupils, neither would he bind himself to give regular lessons at stated periods. He wished to avoid obligations as far as possible, and to feel free to leave Weimar for short periods when so inclined—in other words, to go and come as he liked. His idea was that the pupils whom he accepted should all be far enough advanced to practise and prepare themselves without routine instruction, and he expected them to be ready whenever he gave them an opportunity to play. The musical opportunities of Weimar were such as to afford ample encouragement to any serious-minded young student. Many distinguished musicians, poets, and literary men were constantly coming to visit Liszt. He was fond of entertaining, and liked to have his pupils at hand so that they might join him in entertaining and paying attention to his

guests. He had only three pupils at the
time of which I write, namely, Karl Klindworth from Hanover, Dionys Pruckner
from Munich, and the American whose
musical memories are here presented.
Joachim Raff, however, we regarded as
one of us, for although not at the time a
pupil of Liszt, he had been in former years,
and was now constantly in association with
the master, acting frequently in the capacity of private secretary. Hans von
Bülow had left Weimar not long before my
arrival, and was then on his first regular
concert-tour. Later he returned occasionally for short visits, and I became well
acquainted with him. We constituted, as
it were, a family, for while we had our
own apartments in the city, we all enjoyed the freedom of the two lower rooms
in Liszt's home, and were at liberty to
come and go as we liked. Regularly on
every Sunday at eleven o'clock, with rare
exceptions, the famous Weimar String
Quartet played for an hour and a half or
so in these rooms, and Liszt frequently
joined them in concerted music, old and

new. Occasionally one of the boys would
take the pianoforte part. The quartet-
players were Laub, first violin ; Störr, second violin ; Walbrühl, viola ; and Cossmann, violoncello. Before Laub's time
Joachim had been concertmeister, but he
left Weimar in 1853 and went to Hanover,
where he occupied a similar position. He
occasionally visited Weimar, however,
and would then at times play with the
quartet. Henri Wieniawski, who spent
some months in Weimar, would occasionally take the first violin. My favorite as
a quartet-player was Ferdinand Laub,
with whom I was intimately acquainted,
and I find that the greatest violinists of
the present time hold him in high estimation, many of them regarding him as
the greatest of all quartet-players. We
were always quite at our ease in those
lower rooms, but on ceremonial occasions
we were invited up-stairs to the drawing-
room, where Liszt had his favorite Érard.
We were thus enjoying the best music,
played by the best artists. In addition
to this there were the symphony concerts

and the opera, with occasional attendance at rehearsal. Liszt took it for granted that his pupils would appreciate these remarkable advantages and opportunities and their usefulness, and I think we did.

### THE ALTENBURG

LISZT'S private studio, where he wrote and composed, was at the back of the main building in a lower wing, and may easily be distinguished in the picture by the awnings over the windows. I was not in this room more than half a dozen times during my stay in Weimar, and one of these I remember as the occasion of Liszt's playing the Beethoven "Kreutzer Sonata" with Remenyi, the Hungarian violinist, and giving him a lesson in conception and style of performance. Remenyi was a violinist of fine musical talent, but not a classicist, his style being after the fashion of the class represented by Ole Bull. He was, as is well known, a genuine Hungarian, thoroughly at home in the musical characteristics of his native

country.  He was unconsciously disposed
to color and mark the music of all composers with Hungarian peculiarities, and
this habit gave rise to a story about his
treatment of the concluding strain of the
first theme in the slow movement of the
"Kreutzer Sonata," namely, that, forget-
ting himself, he added to Beethoven's
music the peculiar Hungarian termina-
tion,

as a final ornament.   Whether this story
is true or not, it was widely circulated
and caused a great deal of merriment all
over Germany.

The picture gives a very good view of
the house as it appeared in 1853–54.   In
the nearest corner of the building were
the two large rooms on the ground floor
to which reference has already been made,
of which we boys had the freedom at all
times, and where strangers were uncere-
moniously received.   The Fürstin Sayn-
Wittgenstein had apartments, I think, on

the *bel étage* with her daughter, the Prinzessin Marie.    Any one who was to be honored with an introduction to them was taken to a reception-room up-stairs ; adjoining this was the dining-room.    This print is from a water-color painted for me by my friend Mr. Thomas Allen of Boston. It is copied from a photograph of the original,—a water-color by Carl Hoffman, —which Mr. Hoffman painted expressly for his friend Mr. James M. Tracy, a former pupil of Liszt, who is now a professional pianist and teacher in Denver, Colorado, and to whom I am indebted for permission to publish it here.    Mr. Tracy writes me that it has been published before, but without his permission.

We boys saw little of the Wittgensteins, and I remember dining with them only once.    I sat next to the Princess Marie, who spoke English very well, and it may have been due to her desire to exercise in the language that I was honored with a seat next to her.    Rubinstein met her when he was at Weimar (I shall have more to tell of his visit later), and com-

posed a nocturne which he dedicated to
her. When he came to this country in
1873 he told me that he had met her
again some years later at the palace in
Vienna, but that she had become haughty,
and had not been inclined to pay much
attention to him. There are many Wittgensteins in Russia. When I was in
Wiesbaden in 1879–80 I saw half a dozen
Russian princes of that name. There was
but one Rubinstein.

Liszt had the pick of all the young
musicians in Europe for his pupils, and I
attribute his acceptance of me somewhat
to the fact that I came all the way from
America, something more of an undertak-
ing in those days than it is now. I became very well acquainted with those
whom I have mentioned, especially with
Klindworth and Raff, and before many
days we were all "Dutzbrüder."

The first evening Raff, whom I had
previously never heard of, struck me as
being rather conceited ; but when I grew
to know him better, and realized how
talented he was, I was quite ready to

THE ALTENBURG, LISZT'S HOUSE AT WEIMAR

make allowance for his little touch of self-esteem. We became warm friends, dining together every day at the table d'hôte, and after dinner walking for an hour or so in the park. Nineteen years later I went abroad again and visited Raff at the Conservatory in Frankfort. He interrupted his lessons the moment that he heard I was there, came running downstairs, threw his arms around my neck, and was so overjoyed at seeing me that I felt as if we were boys once more at Weimar. Of the pupils and of the many musicians who came to Weimar to visit Liszt at that time,—"die goldene Zeit" (the Golden Age), as it is still called at Weimar,—I think Klindworth and I are the only survivors. Klindworth is one of the most distinguished teachers in Europe, and taught for many years at the Conservatory in Moscow. He is now in Berlin.

## HOW LISZT TAUGHT

WHAT I had heard in regard to Liszt's method of teaching proved to be abso-

lutely correct. He never taught in the
ordinary sense of the word. During the
entire time that I was with him I did not
see him give a regular lesson in the peda-
gogical sense. He would notify us to
come up to the Altenburg. For instance,
he would say to me, "Tell the boys to
come up to-night at half-past six or seven."
We would go there, and he would call on
us to play. I remember very well the
first time I played to him after I had
been accepted as a pupil. I began with
the "Ballade" of Chopin in A flat major ;
then I played a fugue by Handel in E
minor.

After I was well started he began to
get excited. He made audible suggestions, inciting me to put more enthusiasm
into my playing, and occasionally he
would push me gently off the chair and
sit down at the piano and play a phrase
or two himself by way of illustration.
He gradually got me worked up to such
a pitch of enthusiasm that I put all the
grit that was in me into my playing.

I found at this first lesson that he was

very fond of strong accents in order to mark off periods and phrases, and he talked so much about strong accentuation that one might have supposed that he would abuse it, but he never did. When he wrote to me later about my own piano method, he expressed the strongest approval of the exercises on accentuation.

### "PLAY IT LIKE THIS"

WHILE I was playing to him for the first time, he said on one of the occasions when he pushed me from the chair : "Don't play it that way. Play it like this." Evidently I had been playing ahead in a steady, uniform way. He sat down, and gave the same phrases with an accentuated, elastic movement, which let in a flood of light upon me. From that one experience I learned to bring out the same effect, where it was appropriate, in almost every piece that I played. It eradicated much that was mechanical, stilted, and unmusical in my playing, and developed an elasticity of touch which has lasted all my life, and which I have always tried to impart to my pupils.

At this first lesson I must have played for two or three hours. For some reason or other Raff was not present, but Klindworth and Pruckner were there. They lounged on a sofa and smoked, and I remember wondering if they appreciated the nice time they were having at my ordeal. However, not many days afterward came my opportunity to light a cigar and lounge about the room while Liszt put them through their paces.

Two or three hours is not a long time for a professional musician to practise, and I had often spent many more hours at the piano, but never under such strong incitement. I was exceedingly tired afterward, and actually felt stiff the next day, as if I had performed some very arduous physical work. Liszt heard of this, and turned it into a joke, telling people that at the time set for the next lesson I appeared at the Altenburg with my hand in a sling, and said that I had

strained my wrist while hunting, and
would be unable to play. I think this
is *non è ver e ben trovato,* as I have no
recollection of it.

## LISZT IN 1854

THE best impression of Liszt's appearance
at that time is conveyed by the picture
which shows him approaching the Altenburg. His back is turned; nevertheless,
there is a certain something which shows
the man as he was better even than those
portraits in which his features are clearly
reproduced. The picture gives his gait,
his figure, and his general appearance.
There is his tall, lank form, his high hat
set a little to one side, and his arm a trifle
akimbo. He had piercing eyes. His hair
was very dark, but not black. He wore
it long, just as he did in his older days.
It came almost down to his shoulders, and
was cut off square at the bottom. He had
it cut frequently, so as to keep it at about
the same length. That was a point about
which he was very particular.

HIS FASCINATION

As I remember his hands, his fingers were lean and thin, but they did not impress me as being very long, and he did not have such a remarkable stretch on the keyboard as one might imagine. He was always neatly dressed, generally appearing in a long frock-coat, until he became the Abbé Liszt, after which he wore the distinctive black gown. His general manner and his face were most expressive of his feelings, and his features lighted up when he spoke. His smile was simply charming. His face was peculiar. One could hardly call it handsome, yet there was in it a subtle something that was most attractive, and his whole manner had a fascination which it is impossible to describe.

I remember little incidents which are in themselves trivial, but which illustrate some character-trait. One day Liszt was reading a letter in which a musician was referred to as a certain Mr. So-and-so. He read that phrase over two or three times, and then substituted his own name for that of the musician mentioned, and repeated several times, "A *certain* Mr. Liszt, a *certain* Mr. Liszt, a *certain* Mr. Liszt," adding : "I don't know that that would offend me. I don't know that I should object to being called 'a *certain* Mr. Liszt.'" As he said this his face had an expression of curiosity, as though he were wondering whether he really would be offended or not. But at the same time there was in his face that look of kindness I saw there so often, and I really believe he would not have felt injured by such a reference to himself. There was nothing petty in his feelings.

### LISZT'S INDIGNATION

On one occasion, however, I saw Liszt grow very much excited over what he considered an imposition. One evening he said to us : "Boys, there is a young man coming here to-morrow who says he can play Beethoven's 'Sonata in B Flat, Op. 106.' I want you all three to be here."

We were there at the appointed hour. The pianist proved to be a Hungarian, whose name I have forgotten.

He sat down and began to play in a conveniently slow tempo the bold chords with which the sonata opens. He had not progressed more than half a page when Liszt stopped him, and seating himself at the piano, played in the correct tempo, which was much faster, to show him how the work should be interpreted. "It 's nonsense for you to go through this sonata in that fashion," said Liszt, as he rose from the piano and left the room.

The pianist, of course, was very much disconcerted. Finally he said, as if to console himself: "Well, he can't play it through like that, and that 's why he stopped after half a page."

This sonata is the only one which the composer himself metronomized, and his direction is M.M. $\wp = 138$. A less rapid tempo, $\wp = 100$ or thereabouts, would seem to be more nearly correct, but the pianist took it at a much slower rate than even this.

When the young man left I went out
with him, partly because I felt sorry for
him, he had made such a fiasco, and partly
because I wished to impress upon him the
fact that Liszt could play the whole movement in the tempo in which he began it.
As I was walking along with him, he said,
"I 'm out of money ; won't you lend me
three louis d'or ? "

A day or two later I told Liszt by the
merest chance that the hero of the Op.
106 fiasco had tried to borrow money of
me. "B-r-r-r !  What ? " exclaimed Liszt.
Then he jumped up, walked across the
room, seized a long pipe that hung from
a nail on the wall, and brandishing it as
if it were a stick, stamped up and down
the room in almost childish indignation,
exclaiming, "Drei louis d'or !   Drei louis
d'or ! "   The point is, however, that Liszt
regarded the man as an artistic impostor.
He had sent word to Liszt that he could
play the great Beethoven sonata, not an
inconsiderable feat in those days.   He had
been received on that basis.   He had
failed miserably.   To this artistic imposi-

tion he had added the effrontery of en-
deavoring to borrow money from some one
whom he had met under Liszt's roof.

### OBJECTS TO MY EYE-GLASSES

I HAVE mentioned that Liszt was careful
in his dress. He was also particular about
the appearance of his pupils. I remember
two instances which show how particular
he was in little matters. I have been
near-sighted all my life, and when I went
to Weimar I wore eye-glasses, much pre-
ferring them to spectacles. Eye-glasses
were not much worn in Germany at that
time, and were considered about as affected as the mode of wearing a monocle.
The Germans wore spectacles. I had not
been in Weimar long when Liszt said
to me : "Mason, I don't like to see you
wearing those glasses. I shall send my
optician to fit your eyes with spectacles."

I hardly thought that he was serious,
and so paid no attention to him. But,
sure enough, about a week later there
was a knock at my door, and the optician

presented himself, saying he had come at
the command of Dr. Liszt to examine my
eyes and fit a pair of spectacles to them.
As I was evidently to have no say in the
matter, I submitted, and a few days later
I received two pairs, one in a green and
one in a red case.  I thought them extremely unbecoming, but I was very particular to put them on whenever I went
to see Liszt.

Not long afterward Liszt went to Paris,
and when we called to see him after his
return, and he was talking about his ex-
periences there, he said casually : "By the
way, Mason, I find that gentlemen in Paris
are wearing eye-glasses now.   In fact,
they are considered quite *comme il faut*,
so I have no objection to your wearing
yours."   As he did not ask me to send him
the spectacles, I kept them, and have them
to this day.

Klindworth, Pruckner, and  I  had
played the Bach triple concerto in a
concert at the town hall, and had been
requested to repeat it at an evening concert at the ducal palace.   An hour before

the ducal carriage arrived to take me to the concert, a servant came from the Altenburg with a package which he said Liszt had requested him to be sure to deliver to me. On opening it, I found two or three white ties. It was a hint to me from Liszt that I must dress suitably to play at court.

This incident shows the care that Liszt bestowed on little things relating to the customs and amenities of social life. He evidently sent the ties as a precautionary measure. Possibly he was not sure whether Americans were civilized enough to wear white ties with evening dress, and was afraid I might appear in a red-white-and-blue one. Seriously, however, it was very kind of him to think of a little thing like this.

### A MUSICAL BREAKFAST

BEFORE I went to Weimar I had not been of a very sociable disposition. At Weimar I had to be. Liszt liked to have us about him. He wished us to meet great

men.  He would send us word when he
expected visitors, and sometimes he would
bring them down to our lodgings to see
us.  In every way he tried to make our
surroundings as pleasant as possible.  It
would have been strange if, under such
circumstances, we had not derived some
benefit from our intercourse with our
great master and his visitors.

I shall always recall with amusement a
breakfast which, at Liszt's request, Klindworth and I gave to Joachim and Wieniawski, the violinists, then, of course, very
young men, and to several other distinguished visitors.  Liszt had been entertaining them for several days.  We knew
that it was about time for him to bring
them down to see one of us.  So I was not
surprised when he turned to me one evening and said, "Mason, I want you and
Klindworth to give us a breakfast to-morrow."  I asked him what we should have.
"Oh," he replied, "some *Semmel* [rolls],
caviar, herring," etc.

The next morning Liszt and his visitors
came.  I remember looking out of my

window and watching them cross the ducal park, over the long foot-path which ended directly opposite the house where Klindworth and I lived. It had been raining, and the path was slippery, so that their footsteps were somewhat uncertain.

The breakfast passed off all right. When he had finished, Liszt said, "Now let us take a stroll in the garden." This garden was about four times as large as the back yard of a New York house, and it was unflagged and, of course, muddy from the rain of the previous night. Never shall I forget the sight of Liszt, Joachim, Wieniawski, and our other distinguished guests "strolling" through this garden, wading in mud two inches deep.

### LISZT'S PLAYING

TIME and again at Weimar I heard Liszt play. There is absolutely no doubt in my mind that he was the greatest pianist of the nineteenth century. Liszt was what the Germans call an *Erscheinung*—an

epoch-making genius. Taussig is reported
to have said of him : "Liszt dwells alone
upon a solitary mountain-top, and none
of us can approach him." Rubinstein
said to Mr. William Steinway in the year
1873 : "Put all the rest of us together and
we would not make one Liszt." This was
doubtless hyperbole, but nevertheless
significant as expressing the enthusiasm
of pianists universally conceded to be of
the highest rank. There have been other
great pianists, some of whom are now living, but I must dissent from those writers
who affirm that any of these can be placed
upon a level with Liszt. Those who make
this assertion are too young to have heard
Liszt other than in his declining years,
and it is unjust to compare the playing of
one who has long since passed his prime
with that of one who is still in it. In
the year 1873 Rubinstein told Theodore
Thomas that it was fully worth while to
make a trip to Europe to hear Liszt play ;
but he added : "Make haste and go at
once ; he is already beginning to break
up, and his playing is not up to the stan-

dard of former years, although his personality is as attractive as ever."

In March, 1895, Stavenhagen and Remenyi were dining at my house one evening, and the former began to speak in enthusiastic terms of Liszt's playing. Remenyi interrupted with emphasis: "You have never heard Liszt play—that is, as Liszt used to play in his prime"; and he appealed to me for corroboration, but, unhappily, I never met Liszt again after leaving Weimar in July, 1854.

The difference between Liszt's playing and that of others was the difference between creative genius and interpretation. His genius flashed through every pianistic phrase, it illuminated a composition to its innermost recesses, and yet his wonderful effects, strange as it must seem, were produced without the advantage of a genuinely musical touch.

I remember on one occasion Schulhoff came to Weimar and played in the drawing-room of the Altenburg house. His playing and Liszt's were in marked contrast. He has been mentioned in an earlier chapter as a parlor pianist of high excellence. His compositions, exclusively in the smaller forms, were in great favor and universally played by the ladies.

Liszt played his own "Bénédiction de Dieu dans la Solitude," as pathetic a piece, perhaps, as he ever composed, and of which he was very fond. Afterward Schulhoff, with his exquisitely beautiful touch, produced a quality of tone more beautiful than Liszt's; but about the latter's performance there was intellectuality and the indescribable impressiveness of genius, which made Schulhoff's playing, with all its beauty, seem tame by contrast.

I was not surprised to hear from Theodore Thomas what Rubinstein had told him concerning Liszt's "breaking up," for as far back as the days of "die goldene Zeit" it had seemed to me that there were certain indications in his playing which warranted the belief that his mechanical powers would begin to wane at a comparatively early period in his career. There was too little pliancy, flexion, and relaxation in his muscles; hence a lack of economy in the expenditure of his energies.

He was aware of this, and said in effect on one occasion, as I learned indirectly through either Klindworth or Pruckner: "You are to learn all you can from my playing, relating to conception, style, phrasing, etc., but do not imitate my touch, which, I am well aware, is not a good model to follow. In early years I was not patient enough to 'make haste slowly'—thoroughly to develop in an orderly, logical, and progressive way. I was impatient for immediate results, and took short cuts, so to speak, and jumped through sheer force of will to the goal of my ambition. I wish now that I had progressed by logical steps instead of by leaps. It is true that I have been successful, but I do not advise you to follow my way, for you lack my personality."

In saying this Liszt had no idea of magnifying himself; but it was nevertheless genius which enabled him to accomplish certain results which were out of the ordinary course, and in a way which others,

being differently constituted, could not
follow.  His advice to his pupils was to
be deliberate, and through care and close
attention to important, although seemingly insignificant, details to progress in
an orderly way toward a perfect style.

Notwithstanding this caution, and fall-
ing into the usual tendency of pupils to
imitate the idiosyncrasies and manner-
isms, even faults or weak points, of the
teacher, some of the boys, in their effort
to attain Lisztian effects, acquired a hard
and unsympathetic touch, and thus produced mere noise in the place of full and
resonant tones.

Before going to Weimar I had heard in
various places in Germany that Liszt
spoiled all of those pupils who went to
him without a previously acquired knowledge of method and a habit of the correct
use of the muscles in producing musical
effects.  It was necessary for the pupil to
have an absolutely sure foundation to
benefit by Liszt's instruction.  If he had
that preparation Liszt could develop the
best there was in him.

There is danger of unduly magnifying the importance of a mere mechanical technic. In Liszt's earlier days he inclined in this direction, and wrote the "Études d'Exécution Transcendante." I remember his saying to his pupils one day, when these were the subject of our conversation, that having completed them, his interest in that direction had ceased and he wrote no more. Moreover, he added, "I expected that some day a pianist would appear who would make this subject his specialty, and would accomplish difficulties that were seemingly impossible to perform." It has been said of Liszt that he worshiped this kind of technic. I think the assertion does him injustice. A friend of mine who visited him in Weimar about the year 1858 wrote that Liszt, speaking of one of his pupils, said : "What I like about So-and-so is that he is not a mere 'finger virtuoso' : he does not worship the keyboard of the pianoforte ; it is not his patron saint, but simply the altar before which he pays homage to the idea of the tone-composer." A perfect technic

is more than a wonderful power of pres-
tidigitation, or facility in the manipulation of an instrument. It implies qualities of mind and heart which are essential
to an all-round musical development and
the ability to give them adequate expression.

LISZT AND PIXIS

IN his concertizing days Liszt always
played without the music before him,
although this was not the usual custom
of his time ; and in this connection I
remember an anecdote told to me by
Theimer, one of Dreyschock's assistant
teachers.    Pixis was an old-fashioned
player of considerable reputation in his
day, and was the composer of chamber-
music, besides pianoforte pieces.    Among
other works of his was a duo for two pianofortes.    While this composition was yet
in manuscript it was played in one of the
concerts of Pixis with the assistance of
Liszt.    Pixis, knowing Liszt's habit of
playing from memory, requested him on
this occasion at least to have the music

open before him on the piano-desk, as he himself did not like to risk playing his part without notes, and he felt it would produce an unfavorable impression on the public if Liszt should play from memory while he, the composer, had to rely on his copy. Liszt, as the story goes, made no promise one way or the other. So when the time came the pianists walked on the stage, each carrying his roll of music. Pixis carefully unrolled his and placed it on the piano-desk. Liszt, however, sat down at the piano, and, just before beginning to play, tossed his roll over behind the instrument and proceeded to play his part by heart. Liszt was young at that time, and—well—somewhat inconsiderate. Later on he very rarely played even his own compositions without having the music before him, and during most of the time I was there copies of his later publications were always lying on the piano, and among them a copy of the "Bénédiction de Dieu dans la Solitude," which Liszt had used so many times when playing to his guests that it became associated with memories of Berlioz, Rubinstein, Vieuxtemps, Wieniawski, Joachim, and our immediate circle, Raff, Bülow, Cornelius, Klindworth, Pruckner, and others. When I left Weimar I took this copy with me as a souvenir, and still have it; and I treasure it all the more for the marks of usage which it bears. I also have a very old copy of the Handel "E Minor Fugue," which was given to me by Dreyschock and which I studied with him and afterward with Liszt. Dreyschock had evidently used this same copy when he studied the fugue under Tomaschek. It has penciled figures indicating the fingering, made by both Dreyschock and Liszt. A few years ago I missed this valuable relic for a while, and was much grieved by my loss. Fortunately it was discovered in the ash-barrel at the back of the house. Shades of Tomaschek, Dreyschock, and Liszt!

### LISZT CONDUCTING

IN his conducting Liszt was not unerring. I do not know how far he may have progressed in later years, but when I was in Weimar he had very little practice as a conductor, and was not one of the highest class.  He conducted, however, and with good results on certain important occasions, such as, for instance, when "Lohengrin" was produced.

On account of his strong advocacy of Wagner and modern music generally, he had many enemies, as was to be expected of a man of his prominence.  If perchance a mishap occurred during his conducting there were always petty critics on hand to take advantage of the opportunity and to magnify the fault.

One of these occasions happened at the musical festival at Karlsruhe in October, 1853, while he was conducting Beethoven's "Eroica Symphony."  In a passage where the trombone enters on an off beat the player made a mistake and came in on the even beat.  This error, not the conductor's fault, occasioned such confusion that Liszt was obliged to stop the orchestra and begin over again, and the little fellows made the most of this royal opportunity to pitch into him.

LISZT'S SYMPHONIC POEMS—
REHEARSING "TASSO"

WHEN Liszt first began his career as an
orchestral composer two parties were
formed, one of which predicted success,
the other disaster.  The latter asserted
that he was too much of a pianist and
began too late in life for success in this
direction.  Even in Weimar, in his own
household, so to speak, opinions were di-
vided.  I remember one of my fellow-
pupils saying that he did not think it was
his forte.  Raff had pretty much the same
opinion, and I inclined to agree with
them.  Liszt was in earnest, however, and
availed himself of every means of preparation for the work.  Frequently upon his
request the best orchestral players came
to the Altenburg, and he asked them
about their instruments, their nature, and
whether certain passages were idiomatic
to them.  About the time I came to Weimar to study with him he had nearly
finished "Tasso," and before giving it the
last touches he had a rehearsal of it, which
we attended.  We went to the theater,

and he took the orchestra into a room
which would just about hold it.   Imagine
the din in that room !   The effect was far
from musical, but to Liszt it was the key
to the polyphonic effects which he wished
to produce.

### EXTRACTS FROM A DIARY

As an illustration of some of the advantages of a residence at Weimar almost *en
famille* with Liszt during "die goldene
Zeit," a few extracts from my diary are
presented, showing how closely events
followed one upon another :

"Sunday, April 24, 1853.   At the Altenburg this forenoon at eleven o'clock.
Liszt played with Laub and Cossmann two
trios by César Franck."

This is peculiarly interesting in view of
the fact that the composer, who died about
ten years ago, is just beginning to receive
due appreciation.   In Paris at the present
time there is almost a César Franck cult,
but it is quite natural that Liszt, with his
quick and far-seeing appreciation, should

have taken especial delight in playing his music forty-seven years ago. Liszt was very fond of it.

"May 1. Quartet at the Altenburg at eleven o'clock, after which Wieniawski played with Liszt the violin and pianoforte 'Sonata in A' by Beethoven."

"May 3. Liszt called at my rooms last evening in company with Laub and Wieniawski. Liszt played several pieces, among them my 'Amitié pour Amitié.'"

"May 6. The boys were all at the Hotel Erbprinz this evening. Liszt came in and added to the liveliness of the occasion."

"May 7. At Liszt's, this evening, Klindworth, Laub, and Cossmann played a piano trio by Spohr, after which Liszt played his recently composed sonata and one of his concertos. In the afternoon I had played during my lesson with Liszt the 'C Sharp Minor Sonata' of Beethoven and the 'E Minor Fugue' by Handel."

"May 17. Lesson from Liszt this evening. Played Scherzo and Finale from Beethoven's 'C Sharp Minor Sonata.'"

"May 20, Friday.    Attended a court concert this evening which Liszt conducted.    Joachim played a violin solo by Ernst."

"May 22.    Went to the Altenburg at eleven o'clock this forenoon.    There were about fifteen persons present—quite an unusual thing.    Among other things, a string quartet of Beethoven was played, Joachim taking the first violin."

"May 23.    Attended an orchestral rehearsal at which an overture and a violin concerto by Joachim were performed, the latter played by Joachim."

"May 27.    Joachim Raff's birthday. Klindworth and I presented ourselves to him early in the day and stopped his composing, insisting on having a holiday. Our celebration of this event included a ride to Tiefurt and attendance at a garden concert."

"May 29, Sunday.    At Liszt's this forenoon as usual.    No quartet to-day.    Wieniawski played first a violin solo by Ernst, and afterward with Liszt the latter's duo on Hungarian airs."

"May 30.   Attended a ball of the Er-
holung Gesellschaft this evening.   At our
supper-table were Liszt, Raff, Wieniawski,
Pruckner, and Klindworth.   Got home at
four o'clock in the morning."

"June 4.   Dined with Liszt at the Erbprinz.   Liszt called at my rooms later in
the afternoon, bringing with him Dr.
Marx and lady from Berlin, also Raff and
Winterberger.   Liszt played three Chopin
nocturnes and a scherzo of his own.   In
the evening we were all invited to the
Altenburg.   He played 'Harmonies du
Soir, No. 2,' and his own sonata.   He was
at his best and played divinely."

"June 9.   Had a lesson from Liszt this
evening.   I played Chopin's 'E Minor
Concerto.'"

"June 10.   Went to Liszt's this evening
to a bock-beer soirée.   The beer was a
present to Liszt from Pruckner's father,
who has a large brewery in Munich."

"Sunday, June 12.   Usual quartet forenoon at the Altenburg.   'Quartet, Op.
161,' of Schubert's was played, also one of
Beethoven's quartets."

The last entry may not seem to be particularly important, but it may be as well not to end the quotations from a musical diary with a reference to a bock-beer soirée.

### OPPORTUNITIES

THE period covered by these extracts was chosen at random, and they give a fair idea of the many musical opportunities which were constantly recurring throughout the entire year.

Ferdinand Laub, the leader of the quartet, was about twenty-one years of age, and already a violinist of the first rank.

Wieniawski and Joachim, young men of the age of twenty-two and nineteen years respectively, were among the most welcome visitors to Weimar. Joachim, already celebrated as a quartet-player, was regarded by some as the greatest living violinist. The playing of Wieniawski appealed to me more than that of any other violinist of the time, and I remember it now with intense pleasure.

## BRAHMS IN 1853

On one evening early in June, 1853, Liszt sent us word to come up to the Altenburg next morning, as he expected a visit from a young man who was said to have great talent as a pianist and composer, and whose name was Johannes Brahms. He was to come accompanied by Eduard Remenyi.

The next morning, on going to the Altenburg with Klindworth, we found Brahms and Remenyi already in the reception-room with Raff and Pruckner. After greeting the newcomers, of whom Remenyi was known to us by reputation, I strolled over to a table on which were lying some manuscripts of music. They were several of Brahms's yet unpublished compositions, and I began turning over the leaves of the uppermost in the pile. It was the piano solo "Op. 4, Scherzo, E Flat Minor," and, as I remember, the writing was so illegible that I thought to myself that if I had occasion to study it I should be obliged first to make a copy of it. Finally Liszt came down, and after some general conversation he turned to Brahms and said : "We are interested to hear some of your compositions whenever you are ready and feel inclined to play them."

### NERVOUS BEFORE LISZT

BRAHMS, who was evidently very nervous, protested that it was quite impossible for him to play while in such a disconcerted state, and, notwithstanding the earnest solicitations of both Liszt and Remenyi, could not be persuaded to approach the piano.    Liszt, seeing that no progress was being made, went over to the table, and taking up the first piece at hand, the illegible scherzo, and saying, "Well, I shall have to play," placed the manuscript on the piano-desk.

We had often witnessed his wonderful feats in sight-reading, and regarded him as infallible in that particular, but, notwithstanding our confidence in his ability, both Raff and I had a lurking dread of the possibility that something might happen which would be disastrous to our unquestioning faith. So, when he put the scherzo on the piano-desk, I trembled for the result. But he read it off in such a marvelous way—at the same time carrying on a running accompaniment of audible criticism of the music—that Brahms was amazed and delighted. Raff thought, and so expressed himself, that certain parts of this scherzo suggested the Chopin "Scherzo in B Flat Minor," but it seemed to me that the likeness was too slight to deserve serious consideration. Brahms said that he had never seen or heard any of Chopin's compositions. Liszt also played a part of Brahms's "C Major Sonata, Op. 1."

### DOZING WHILE LISZT PLAYED

A LITTLE later some one asked Liszt to play his own sonata, a work which was quite recent at that time, and of which he was very fond. Without hesitation, he sat down and began playing. As he progressed he came to a very expressive part of the sonata, which he always imbued

with extreme pathos, and in which he
looked for the especial interest and sympathy of his listeners.    Casting a glance
at Brahms, he found that the latter was
dozing in his chair.    Liszt continued playing to the end of the sonata, then rose and
left the room.    I was in such a position
that Brahms was hidden from my view,
but I was aware that something unusual
had taken place, and I think it was Remenyi who afterward told me what it
was.    It is very strange that among the
various accounts of this Liszt-Brahms
first interview—and there are several—
there is not one which gives an accurate
description of what took place on that
occasion ; indeed, they are all far out of
the way.    The events as here related are
perfectly clear in my own mind, but not
wishing to trust implicitly to my memory
alone, I wrote to my friend Klindworth,
—the only living witness of the incident
except myself, as I suppose,—and requested him to give an account of it as
he remembered it.    He corroborated my
description in every particular, except

that he made no specific reference to the
drowsiness of Brahms, and except, also,
that, according to my recollection, Brahms
left Weimar on the afternoon of the day
on which the meeting took place ; Klindworth writes that it was on the morning
of the following day—a discrepancy of
very little moment.

Brahms and Remenyi were on a concert
tour at the time of which I write, and
were dependent on such pianos as they
could find in the different towns in which
they appeared.    This was unfortunate,
and sometimes brought them into extreme
dilemma.    On one occasion the only piano
at their disposal was just a half-tone at
variance with the violin.    There was no
pianoforte-tuner at hand, and although
the violin might have been adapted to the
piano temporarily, Remenyi would have
had serious objections to such a proceeding.    Brahms therefore adapted himself
to the situation, transposed the piano part
to the pitch of the violin, and played the
whole composition, Beethoven's "Kreutzer Sonata," from memory.    Joachim, at-

tracted by this feat, gave Brahms a letter
of introduction to Schumann.  Shortly
after the untoward Weimar incident
Brahms paid a visit to Schumann, then
living in Düsseldorf.  The acquaintance-
ship resulting therefrom led to the famous article of Schumann entitled "Neue
Bahnen," published shortly afterward
(October 23, 1853) in the Leipsic "Neue
Zeitschrift für Musik," which started
Brahms on his musical career.  It is
doubtful if up to that time any article
had made such a sensation throughout
musical Germany.  I remember how utterly the Liszt circle in Weimar were
astounded.  This letter was at first, doubtless, an obstacle in the way of Brahms, but
as it resulted in stirring up great rivalry
between two opposing parties it eventually contributed much to his final success.

### "LOHENGRIN" FOR THE FIRST
### TIME IN LEIPSIC

LISZT never questioned Wagner's sincerity.  He considered "Lohengrin"

Wagner's greatest work up to the time at which it was composed. It was dedicated to Liszt, and, as Raff told me, the good man could not conceive that Wagner would dedicate anything but his best and greatest to his friend and champion, such was Liszt's faith in the struggling composer whose cause he had made his own.[1]

On the occasion of the first performance of a Wagner opera in any neighboring town, a delegation from Weimar was apt to be on hand for the purpose of making propaganda; and this was the case on Saturday, January 7, 1854, when the opera of "Lohengrin" was given in Leipsic for the first time.

We boys were demonstrative claqueurs, and almost always succeeded in making a sensation, especially in a town like Leipsic, where we had acquaintances among the Conservatory students and could get them to help us.

The general public and a large majority

[1] In a letter written twenty-four years later, in 1878, Liszt says of "Parsifal": "The composition of the first act is finished; in it are revealed the most wondrous depths and the most celestial heights of art."

of the musicians were not at all favorably disposed toward Wagner's music in those days, and in this connection a remark of Joachim Raff made to me in 1879–80, on the occasion of my second visit to Germany, was significant. Raff had been in earlier years, perhaps, the most ardent of all pioneers in the Wagner cause. A quarter of a century had elapsed since I had seen Raff, and naturally one of my first questions was, "Raff, how is the Wagner cause?" "Oh," said he, "the public have gone 'way over to the other extreme. You know how hard it was to force Wagner upon them twenty-five years ago, and now they go just as much too far the other way and are unreasonable in their excessive homage." "Well," I replied, "I suppose the matter will find its level and be adjusted as time passes on."

After the performance of "Lohengrin," which, by the way, was successful, the whole Liszt party, by invitation, went to supper at the house of the concertmeister, Ferdinand David. Quite a number of other guests were present. Among them

I remember with pleasure my Boston friends and fellow-townsmen Charles C. Perkins and J. C. D. Parker, who were temporarily located in Leipsic, pursuing their musical studies.

Brahms also was present, and during the evening he played the Andante from his "F Minor Sonata, Op. 5."

### IN STUTTGART—HOTEL MARQUAND

Not long after my visit to Raff in 1879–80 I went on a pleasure trip to Stuttgart, and on account of old associations stopped at the Hotel Marquand. One of the objects of my visit was to meet again my old Weimar fellow-pupil Dionys Pruckner, at that time eminent among the staff of pianoforte teachers in the famous Stuttgart Conservatory of Music. Alighting at the hotel, I was impressed with the marks of consideration shown to me by the hotel porter. He was so very attentive that I was somewhat puzzled. The explanation was apparent the next day when he respectfully inquired if I was the kapell-

meister of New York !  He had read the
name and address on one of my trunks
and jumped at conclusions.  I told him
that I was not that individual, and explained that in New York no such office
existed, although the title might be with
propriety applied to the conductor of the
Philharmonic Society.   However, the
idea found a lodgment in his head, quite
to my advantage, as evidenced by the
many attentions he paid to me throughout my stay.

### THE SCHUMANN "FEIER" IN BONN, 1880

OVER a quarter of a century elapsed after
my first meeting with Brahms before I
saw him again, and then the meeting occurred at Bonn on the Rhine, on May 3,
1880.   He was there, in company with
Joachim and other artists, to take part in
the ceremonies attendant on the unveil-
ing of the Schumann *Denkmal*.

There were also musical performances,
and at a morning recital of chamber-music
the program consisted solely of Schu-

mann's works, vocal and instrumental, with the addition of the Brahms "Violin Concerto," played by Joachim.  The concluding number was Schumann's "Piano Quartet in E Flat Major, Op. 47," Brahms playing the piano part, and Joachim, Heckmann, and Bellman playing respectively violin, viola, and violoncello.

### BRAHMS'S PIANOFORTE-PLAYING

THE pianoforte-playing of Brahms was far from being finished or even musical. His tone was dry and devoid of sentiment, his interpretation inadequate, lacking style and contour.   It was the playing of a composer, and not that of a virtuoso. He paid little if any attention to the marks of expression as indicated by Schumann in the copy.   This was especially and painfully apparent in the opening measures of the first movement.   This introductory passage is marked, "Sostenuto assai," followed by the main movement marked, "Allegro ma non troppo."   Instead of accommodating himself to the

quiet and subdued nature of the introduction, the pianist quite ignored Schumann's
esthetic directions, and began with a
vigorous attack, which was sustained
throughout the movement. The continued force and harshness of his tone
quite overpowered the stringed instruments. As an ensemble the performance
was not a success.

On going home to dinner, and learning
that Brahms was stopping at the hotel, I
gave my card to the porter, with instructions to deliver it to Brahms as soon as he
came in. When about half-way through
the table d'hôte the porter entered and
said that Brahms was in the outer hall,
waiting to see me. He was very cordial. At the moment I had quite forgotten that I had met him at David's
house in Leipsic, so I said : "The last
time I met you was in Weimar on that
very hot day in June, 1853 ; do you remember it ?"

"Very well indeed, and I am glad to
see you again. Just now my time is very
much engaged, but we are going up the

river on a picnic this afternoon—Joachim
and others; will you come along? We
are going to a summer restaurant on the
Rhine, where they have excellent beer,
and it will be *ganz gemütlich.*"

I regretted extremely that I had to
forego the pleasure of this excursion, and
fully realized the opportunity I was losing; but my party—there were four of us,
my wife and I and two children—had
previously arranged our plans, and in
order to make connections we were
obliged to go on to Cologne that day.

Here was a companion-piece to the
disappointment occasioned by my having to forego the pleasure and profit of
a foot-tramp through the Tyrol with
Richard Wagner, as already related in
these "Memories." But so the Fates
ordained.

Partly on account of the untoward Weimar incident, and partly for the sake of
his own individuality, I took a peculiar
interest in Brahms. His work is wonderfully condensed, his constructive power
masterly. By his scholarly development

of themes through augmentation, diminu-
tion, inversion, imitation, and other de-
vices, he seems to be introducing new
thematic material, while the fact is, as
will be seen on close investigation, that
he is presenting the original theme in
varied form and shape, and gradually un-
folding and expanding its possibilities to
the uttermost.   In other words, his treatment is exhaustive and complete.   In his
later piano compositions this is readily
apparent, and as these pieces are short,
and at the same time complete in form,
they furnish excellent opportunities to
the student for analytical studies.   In all
that relates to the intellectual faculty
Brahms is indisputably a master.   I find
this to be the consensus of opinion among
intelligent musicians.   But there are dif-
ferences of opinion as regards his emotional susceptibilities, and it is just this
fact that prevents many from fully ac-
cepting him.   The emotional and intellectual should be in equipoise in order to
attain the highest results, but in the music
of Brahms the latter seems to predomi-

nate. In sympathetic and affectionate treatment, so far as relates to his piano composition, he does not compare with Chopin.

## A HISTORICAL ERROR CORRECTED

I HAVE read in a recent number of a musical magazine the following sentence: "We have seen with what ardor the first compositions of this serious young man [Brahms] were greeted by Schumann and Liszt."

I have already mentioned the fact that all of the published accounts of the first meeting of Liszt and Brahms were far from accurate, and in fact convey an impression directly opposite to the truth; and the foregoing statement, according to my belief, is just as far from being in accordance with the facts. I am quite sure that Liszt was not enthusiastic about Brahms at the time of the first interview in Weimar heretofore described, and the letter received from my friend Karl Klindworth, in Berlin, sustains me in this

belief.   Liszt was of too kindly a disposition to treasure up animosity against
Brahms on account of the mishap on that
occasion ; but the fact that Brahms was
put forward by the anti-Wagnerites as
their champion may possibly have influ-
enced him somewhat.   A coolness also
sprang up between Joachim and Liszt,
although during my stay in Weimar the
violinist had been welcomed so frequently
at the Altenburg.   During the entire
career of Brahms he and Joachim were
close friends.

### MORE ABOUT LISZT'S WONDERFUL SIGHT-READING

LISZT'S playing of the Brahms scherzo
was a remarkable feat, but he was constantly doing almost incredible things in
the way of reading at sight.   Another
instance of his skill in this direction occurs to me and is well worthy of mention.

Raff had composed a sonata for violin
and pianoforte in which there were ever-
varying changes in measure and rhythm ;

measures of $\frac{7}{8}$, $\frac{7}{4}$, $\frac{5}{4}$, alternated with common and triple time, and seemed to mix
together promiscuously and without regard to order.   Notwithstanding this apparent disorder, there was an under-
current, so to speak, of the ordinary $\frac{3}{4}$ or
$\frac{4}{4}$ time, and to the player who could pene-
trate the rhythmic mask the difficulty of
performance quickly vanished.   Raff had
arranged with Laub and Pruckner that
they should practise the sonata together,
and then, on a favorable occasion, play it
in Liszt's presence.   So on one of the
musical mornings at the Altenburg these
gentlemen began to play the sonata.
Pruckner, of sensitive and nervous organization, found the changes of measure
too confusing, especially when played before company, and broke down at the first
page.   Another and yet a third attempt
was made, but with the like result.   Liszt,
whose interest was aroused, exclaimed :
"I wonder if I can play that!"   Then,
taking his place at the instrument, he
played it through at sight in rapid tempo
and without the slightest hesitation.   He

had intuitively divined the regularity of movement which lay beneath the surface.

### LISZT'S MOMENTS OF CONTRITION

DEEP beneath the surface there was in Liszt's organization a religious trend which manifested itself openly now and then, and there were occasions upon which his contrition displayed itself to an inordinate degree. Joachim Raff, long his intimate friend and associate, told me that these periods were sometimes of considerable duration, and while they lasted he would seek solitude, and going frequently to church, would throw himself upon the flagstones before a *Muttergottesbild*, and remain for hours, as Raff expressed it, so deeply absorbed as to be utterly unconscious of events occurring in his presence.

Rubinstein also told me that on one occasion he had been a witness of such an act on the part of Liszt. One afternoon at dusk they were walking together in the cathedral at Cologne, and quite sud-

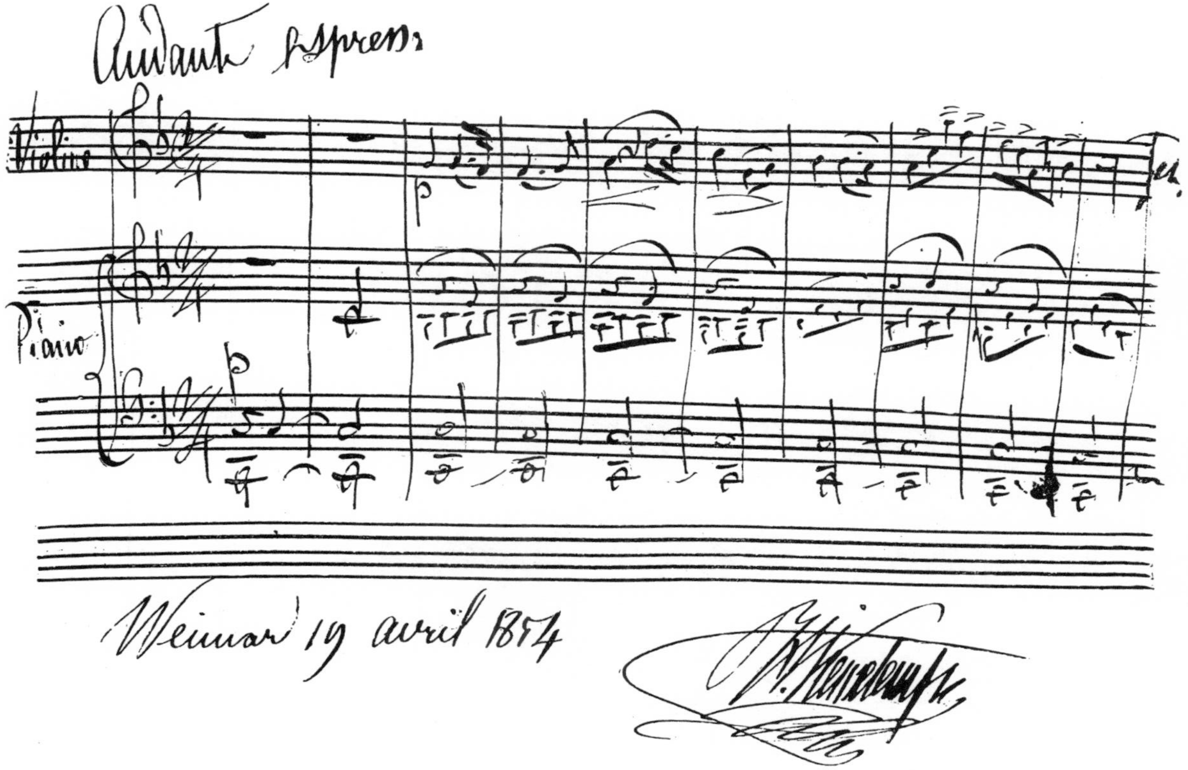
Andante espress.
Violino
Piano
p
Weimar 19 avril 1854

denly Rubinstein missed Liszt, who had disappeared in a mysterious way. He searched for quite a while through the many secluded nooks and corners of the immense building, and finally found Liszt kneeling before a *prie-dieu*, so deeply engrossed that Rubinstein had not the heart to disturb him, and so left the building alone.

### PETER CORNELIUS

SOMETIME, I think late, in 1853 Peter Cornelius, nephew of the celebrated painter of that name, and composer of the comic opera "The Barber of Bagdad," came to Weimar and was added to the Altenburg circle. He was well known and highly esteemed by musicians, and as he was always cheery and bubbling over with musical enthusiasm, I at once became very fond of him as a friend, and later on paid due homage to his decided talent as a composer. As an illustration of how easy it is to underrate the abilities of a new acquaintance the following incident is both interesting and instructive. In October, 1853, or thereabouts, quite a large musical festival took place in Karlsruhe, which was under the general direction of Liszt, who also conducted the orchestra. It goes without saying that under the management of Liszt a number of selections from the Wagner operas were played, and one of these happened to be the bridal chorus from "Lohengrin." Wagner at that time was an entirely new experience to Cornelius, and after the concert, while speaking to Liszt of the beauty of Wagner's music, he instanced this bright and pretty melody, emphasizing its beauty as though it were the special object of his admiration. We boys, while we recognized the beauty of the bridal march and its fitness for the place in which it occurs, were apt to coddle ourselves upon our superior knowledge of Wagner, and would have saved our enthusiasm for the more completed and distinctly Wagnerian characteristics. The enthusiasm of Cornelius for the purely melodic phrases of Wagner, which

were in no wise characteristic of his genius, rather led us to look down upon the
musical perceptions of Cornelius—or perhaps I should speak only for myself and
give these as my personal impressions;
but it was not long before his great talent
was duly recognized and acknowledged,
at least by musicians. Cornelius was a
charming fellow, and I enjoyed his society
because he was so enthusiastically and intensely musical.

### SOME FAMOUS VIOLINISTS

I HAVE already mentioned in these papers
my meeting with Joachim in Leipsic in
the year 1849. He was then about eighteen years of age and already famous as a
violinist. He was of medium height, had
broad, open features, and a heavy shock
of dark hair somewhat like that of Rubinstein. I had a letter of introduction to
him, which I presented a short time after
my arrival in Leipsic, and received immediately a return call from him. He
was kind and affable, and easy to become

acquainted with, but owing to diffidence on my part I did not improve the opportunity as I should have done, a circumstance which I now much regret. He played the Mendelssohn concerto in one of the Gewandhaus concerts within a month of my arrival at Leipsic, and I heard him then for the first time, and was much impressed by his beautiful performance. Subsequently, when in Weimar, I had the pleasure of meeting him on many occasions, for he was in the habit of going there not infrequently, and would sometimes take part in the Altenburg private musicales, as well as in the public concerts at the theater.

During the year 1845–46 I heard and became well acquainted with three famous violinists, Vieuxtemps, Ole Bull, and Sivori, who came to Boston and played many times both in public and in private. They were all great players, each having his special individuality. Vieuxtemps and Ole Bull I met several times in later years, and became familiar with their playing. Vieuxtemps came to Weimar

and played both in private and in public.
His playing was wonderfully precise and
accurate, every tone receiving due attention, and his phrasing was delightful.
Scale and arpeggio passages were absolutely clean and without a flaw. He was
certainly a player of exquisite taste, and
he still preserved his characteristics when
I heard him years later, in 1853 at Weimar, and in 1873 at New York. Ole Bull
came to Boston a year or so after Vieuxtemps. He was a born violinist, and developed after his own fashion and nature,
in the manner of a genius. Vieuxtemps
was the result of scientific training and
close adherence to well-founded principles. Ole Bull, on the other hand, was a
law unto himself, and burst out into full
blossom without showing the various degrees of growth. He did not realize the
importance of close attention to detail
while in the course of development.

Sivori was of the gentle, poetic, and
graceful class of players. Beauty and
grace rather than self-assertion characterized his style. Ernst, whom I heard in

Homburg in the year 1852, was a player of great intensity of feeling, and was regarded as the most fervent violinist of his time. Joachim's style impressed me as classical and rather reserved, and while I enjoyed and admired it, there was present no feeling of enthusiasm. Wilhelmj, with his broad and noble style, was certainly most impressive. Henri Wieniawski had a musical organization of great intensity, and this, combined with his perfect technic, made his playing irresistible. Ferdinand Laub, for some reason not so well known to the general public as he should be, is generally conceded by the most distinguished violinists to have been the greatest of all quartet-players. Laub was concertmeister during the whole period of my stay in Weimar, and was an intimate friend of mine. It will be remembered that at that time Bernhard Cossmann was the violoncellist of the Weimar string quartet. I owe many delightful moments of musical enjoyment to his exquisitely poetical and refined playing. The last time I met him was

With
most respectful and kind feelings

[signature]

Astor House, New York
Nov. 19th 1845.

at his own house in Frankfort. His wife
and children were present, and being thus
quite *en famille*, we played together, for
the sake of old times, the piano and violoncello sonata of Beethoven in A major.

There are many others whom I am
prevented by lack of space from mention-
ing; but I must not omit the name of my
friend Adolf Brodsky, a violinist of the
first rank, and a man of great nobility of
character. His playing is broad, intelligent, and thoroughly musical, whether as
soloist or as first violin in chamber quartet
music. Sometimes I have heard him in
the privacy of my own home, where, feeling entire freedom from restraint, he has
thrown himself intensely into his music,
to my thorough and complete musical
satisfaction.

### REMENYI

I HAVE already had something to say of
Eduard Remenyi, the Hungarian violinist
who accompanied Brahms to Weimar in
1853. He was a talented man, and was

esteemed by Liszt as being, in his way, a
good violinist.  He remained at Weimar
after Brahms left there, and I became intimately acquainted with him.  He was
very entertaining, and so full of fun that
he would have made a tiptop Irishman.
He was at home in the Gipsy music of his
own country, and this was the main characteristic of his playing.  He had also a
fad for playing Schubert melodies on the
violin with the most attenuated pianissimo effects, and occasionally his hearers
would listen intently after the tone had
ceased, imagining that they still heard a
trace of it.

Not long before leaving Weimar I had
some fun with him by asking if he had
ever heard "any bona-fide American
spoken."  He replied that he did not
know there was such a language.  "Well,"
said I, "listen to this for a specimen:
'Ching-a-ling-a-dardee,  Chebung  cum
Susan.'"  I did not meet him again until
1878, twenty-four years after leaving
Weimar.  I was going up-stairs to my
studio in the Steinway building when

some one told me that Remenyi had arrived and was rehearsing for his concerts
in one of the rooms above.   So, going up,
I followed the sounds of the violin, gave
a quick knock, opened the door, and went
in.   Remenyi looked at me for a moment,
rushed forward and seized my hand, and
as he wrung it cried out : "Ching-a-ling-a-
dardee, Chebung cum Susan !"   He had
remembered it all those years.


### SOME DISTINGUISHED OPERA-SINGERS

MY concert-playing and teaching have
naturally made me more interested in
instrumental than in vocal music.   Moreover, the principal celebrities who came
to visit Liszt during my sojourn at Weimar were composers and instrumentalists.
For that reason I met but few distinguished opera-singers during my stay
abroad.   However, I heard the best of
them in opera or concert.

In Boston, about the year 1846–47, the
Havana Italian Opera gave a season at
the Howard Athenæum of that city, and

created considerable interest. They gave, I think for the first time in this country, Verdi's "Ernani," which was received with great favor. The principal soprano was Mme. Fortunata Tedesco, who was afterward at the Grand Opéra in Paris from 1851 to 1857. The tenor was Signore Perelli, who had an exceptionally fine voice. Both of these singers had well-trained voices and were well supported by chorus and orchestra. As this was my first experience in opera, it produced a deep and lasting impression.

The opera season in Leipsic in the year 1852, beginning about the 1st of February and continuing up to the 1st of May, was notable, for it afforded the opportunity of hearing in quick succession three singers of world-wide reputation : Henriette Sontag, Johanna Wagner, and De la Grange.

### HENRIETTE SONTAG

THE singer of whom I have the liveliest impression is Henriette Sontag, whom I heard in Leipsic on her first appearance

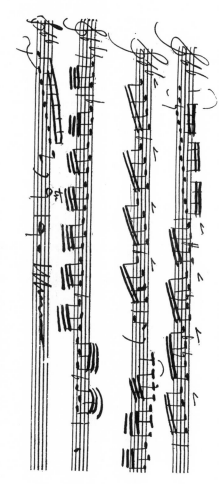

*Henriette Voigt.*
*Sonntag.*

*München den 29. Mai 1839.*

after she had been twenty years in retirement. The interest I took in the occasion was much increased by the fact that I had a seat next to Moscheles, who was very communicative, and gave me an interesting history of his long acquaintance with Sontag, whom he had heard at her last appearance, I think, before her retirement. He was naturally on the *qui vive*, and impatiently waited for the opera to begin. Like many of her other old admirers who were in the theater, he was full of expectancy mingled with dread of possible failure. She appeared as *Maria* in Donizetti's "Fille du Régiment." In this part the voice of the singer is heard before she appears on the stage, and as soon as Moscheles heard Sontag's voice trilling behind the scenes, he exclaimed with delight, "It is Sontag! Nobody I have heard since she left the stage could do that! She is the same Henriette!"

Some of the rôles in which I heard her were *Amina* in "Sonnambula," *Martha* in the opera of that name, *Susan* in "The Marriage of Figaro," and *Rosina* in "The

Barber of Seville." I enjoyed the lovely feminine quality of her voice and manner. There was something peculiarly charming and womanly about her. She sang with unfailing ease and grace, her voice being so flexible that it sounded like the trilling of birds. The most difficult roulades and cadences were given with absolute accuracy and rhythm. It was simply fascinating.

### JOHANNA WAGNER

DURING the month of March of the same year, Johanna Wagner, niece of Richard Wagner, sang in several operas. Among those in which I heard her were Bellini's "Romeo and Juliet," as *Romeo* ; "Fidelio," as *Leonora* or *Fidelio* ; and "Iphigenia in Aulis," by Gluck, as *Iphigenia*. Here indeed she was a contrast to Sontag, and in these parts she seemed to me quite unapproachable. Her voice was large and full, and her acting most dramatic. Like all the German singers whom I heard, she lacked the nicety of detail, the clear and beautiful phrasing, characteristic of the

Italians I had heard in Boston.    But when
I grew to know the German method, I
began to admire it, not so much for the
actual singing itself as for the combination
of qualities that entered into it—the
artistic earnestness, the acting, and the
musicianship.

### MME. DE LA GRANGE

It was my experience that the Germans
themselves greatly admired singing of the
Italian school, for when, following Sontag
and Wagner, Mme. de la Grange came
the next month and sang an engagement
in Leipsic (April and May, 1852), the
management doubled the prices, and, notwithstanding this, the house was crowded
every time she sang.    She was in her
prime, and one of the finest singers I ever
heard.    Her style was brilliant and daz-
zling, but never lacking in repose.    Her
high tones were clear and musical, without any trace of shrillness, and in the
most rapid passages the tones were never
slurred or confused, but distinct and in

perfect rhythmic order. The rôles in which she most appealed to me were as *Queen of the Night* in "The Magic Flute," by Mozart, and *Rosina* in "The Barber of Seville," by Rossini. But she also sang both parts of *Isabella* and *Alice* in Meyerbeer's "Robert the Devil" in the most admirable manner.

### "DER VEREIN DER MURLS"

LISZT was the head and front of the Wagner movement; but except when visitors came to Weimar and were inveigled into an argument by Raff, who was an ardent disciple of the new school, there was but little discussion of the Wagner question. Pruckner started a little society, the object being to oppose the Philistines, or old fogies, and uphold modern ideas. Liszt was the head and was called the Padishah (chief), and the pupils and others, Raff, Bülow, Klindworth, Pruckner, Cornelius, Laub, Cossmann, etc., were "Murls." In a letter to Klindworth, then in London, Liszt writes of Rubinstein: "That is a

clever fellow, the most notable musician,
pianist, and composer who has appeared
to me among the modern lights—with the
exception of the Murls.    Murlship alone
is lacking to him still."    On the manuscript of Liszt's "Sonate" he himself
wrote, "Für die Murlbibliothek."

## THE WAGNER CAUSE IN WEIMAR

My admiration for Wagner did not go to
the extreme of Liszt's and of my fellow-
pupils'.    Liszt rarely expressed his opinion
of Wagner, because he took it for granted
that everybody knew it, and he was not
a controversialist.    I know that he considered those people who refused to follow
Wagner as old fogies, and my colleagues
used to twit me for not being as enthusiastic as they were.    Certain passages in
his operas have always given me great
musical enjoyment and delight, but here
and there are crudities which, as it seemed
to me, were unpardonable in a great composer.    Under these circumstances I could
not pose as a genuine Murl, although this

fact did not disturb the genial and fra-
ternal relations which existed between my
colleagues and me ; and on occasion also
I was equal to the best of them in exercising the specialty of a genuine Murl
claqueur.

I think that Wagner will always rank
among the greatest composers, but will
not always remain as preëminent as he is
now in the popular estimation.   Some of
his compositions are wonderfully intricate, although musical, but at times his
faults appear and disturb the balance of
things in such a way that the music loses the
effect of spontaneity and becomes forced.

In the Weimar days the general objection of the "old fogies" was that his music
lacked melody.    Doubtless by melody
they meant the little tunes of the anti-
Wagner period ; but the fact is that Wagner has contributed his share to increasing
the scope of melody and enlarging its
boundaries.   It may be that he has gone
too far in this direction and has completely obliterated all limitations, thus
approaching dangerously near confusion.

It was said that he had no melody, but his scores are full of it.  There are sometimes so many melodies in combination, each exercising its individuality and proceeding independently, that the "tune effect" is obscured and lost in the crowd of accompanying tunes.  But to me Wagner's melody seems restless.  It comes on suddenly and progresses without periods of repose.  There is almost constant motion, which produces a feeling of unrest.  A sentence must have its commas, semicolons, and periods, and punctuation is as necessary in music as it is in letters.

I have never quite understood just what it is in Wagner's music that so fascinates many people whom I know to be unmusical.

### RAFF IN WEIMAR

OF my Weimar comrades, Joachim Raff, it is hardly necessary to say, became the most distinguished.  My first impression of him was not wholly favorable.  He was hard to become acquainted with and not disposed to meet one half-way.  He was fond of argument, and if one side was taken he was very apt to take the other. He liked nothing better than to get one to commit himself to a proposition and then to attack him with all his resources, which were many. Upon better acquaintance, however, one found a kind heart and faithful friend whose constancy was to be relied on. He was very poor, and there were times when he seemed hardly able to keep body and soul together. Once he was arrested for debt. The room in which he was confined, however, was more comfortable, if anything, than his own. He had a piano, a table, music-paper, and pen and ink sent there. How this was accomplished I do not know, but I think Liszt must have had a hand in it. Raff enjoyed himself composing and playing, and we saw to it that he had good fare. The episode made little impression on him : so long as he could compose he was happy. However, the matter was compromised, and in a short time he returned to his own lodgings. He was a hard worker and composed incessantly, with only a brief interval for dinner and a little exercise. We habitually sat together, and afterward usually took a short walk. I enjoyed his conversation exceedingly and derived much profit from it.

At about five o'clock in the afternoon, looking out of my window, I would frequently see Raff coming over the path leading through the park, with a bundle of manuscript under his arm. He liked to come and play to me what he had composed. His playing was not artistic, because he paid little attention to it, and he did not attempt to elaborate or finish his style.

He composed very rapidly, and many of his compositions do not amount to much. He could not get decent remuneration for good music, and he had to live; therefore he wrote many pieces that were of the jingling sort, because his publishers paid well for them. Sometimes, however, he turned out a composition which was really worthy, and among his works are symphonies, sonatas, trios, and chamber-music which gained him reputation. His symphony "Im Walde" is well known in the musical world, and his "Cavatina" for violin, although not a piece of importance, is one of the most popular and effective violin solos and exists in various arrangements. At times he was much dejected, and there was a dash of bitterness in his disposition. I think he felt that, being obliged to turn out music for a living, he would never attain the rank to which his talents entitled him.

In promoting the cause of Wagner, Raff did considerable work for which Liszt got the credit. I think that at one time Raff acted as Liszt's private secretary ; but he had decided ideas of his own, and knew how to express them. Being generally in close accord with Liszt, and having a ready pen, he rendered great assistance in promulgating the doctrines of the new school by means of essays, brochures, and newspaper articles. Of course much that he wrote was based upon suggestions made by Liszt. Raff was a tower of strength in himself, while at the same time acting as Liszt's mouthpiece in the Wagner propaganda.

### DR. ADOLF BERNHARD MARX

WHEN Dr. Adolf B. Marx of Berlin was in Weimar in June, 1853, it was by invitation of Liszt for the purpose of bringing out a new oratorio which he had just composed. As usual on such occasions, we gave him a warm reception, and Liszt arranged a midday dinner at the Hotel zum Erbprinzen, at which some eight or ten guests were present. In the afternoon we all attended a rehearsal of the oratorio, which lasted from four o'clock until eleven o'clock P.M. According to my present recollections, the work did not have a brilliant success. I was reminded of this event by the receipt of the following letter in March, 1901, from an old friend, Mr. Adolph Stange, who happened to be present on the occasion :

SUWALKI, POLAND, RUSSIA,
24 January, 1901.

DEAR DR. MASON: When you wrote your "Memories of a Musical Life," July–October, 1900, of Century Illustrated Monthly Magazine, you probably did not have any presentiment that there is in a distant country, far from you, somebody who only by one day younger than yourself (born January 25, 1829) will be reading with the greatest interest your excellent and truthful description of different musical celebrities and authorities. Being myself for many years a pupil of Gerke and of Henselt in St. Petersburg, I had been with many of the eminent men you name personally acquainted; with Moscheles and Rubinstein I had more often and more intimate relations, and my delight was naturally great in reading your true and graphic account of some of my former musical friends. It is indeed with a feeling of admiration and gratitude that I am now addressing these lines to its author. Your interesting description of your stay at Weimar in 1853 gave me special pleasure, as in that same year, in May, June, and July, I had also been with Liszt in Weimar, and I remember you, dear Dr. Mason, perfectly, as well as Klindworth, Pruckner, the two Wieniawskis, Winterberger, Raff, and others; they are all living in my memory. That period of my youth is full of the most beautiful and noble impressions.

Your account of that incomparable meister we both, I dare say, equally admire, awakened in me Liszt's greatness as artist, and still more, if I may say so, the greatness of his nature and character, so richly endowed with so many generous and noble instincts; and I recall with

delight to my mind our pleasant walks in the
Schlossgarten, where we visited Klindworth
in his modest apartments; the supper at the
Hotel zum Erbprinzen, where Liszt wished to
get acquainted with the card-game "prefer-
ence," which I had to show him; our visits to
the Schloss, in the ground floor of which we
listened to Liszt's divine playing and afterward got invited to dine up-stairs with the Princess Wittgenstein and her charming daughter.
I believe you had already left Weimar when
Professor Adolf Marx came from Berlin to
visit Liszt and brought with him the score of
his new oratorio.   Marx wished to say a few
words about its performance to Liszt before
the first rehearsal, but was much disappointed,
as he told me, not to find an appropriate moment to speak with the meister, whose attention was constantly taken up by his pupils.
On the day of the rehearsal, Marx, who was
sitting next to me, again expressed his regret
at not having found an opportunity to talk
the matter over with Liszt.   Shortly after the
rehearsal had commenced I felt several times
Marx's elbows, which, giving way to his enthusiasm, came in close and sensible contact
with mine.   At last he exclaimed : "Liszt
guesses my most secret thoughts and intentions in my own composition!" . . .

Let me, dear Dr. Mason, assure you what
real and intense enjoyment I experienced by

the perusal of your "Musical Memories," and beg to thank you from all my heart for giving me the possibility of recalling once over again those dear and ever-present reminiscences of a bygone but ever-delightful time in my life. It is seldom one can read in a biography a description like yours, which expresses in a few words, with so much reality, truthfulness, and impartiality, the characteristics of a whole series of well-known artists. Finally, you will ask: "Stranger, who art thou?" I will not, like *Lohengrin*, make a mystery of it, but answer your question: I wanted to become what you are now! After my return from Weimar, however, where I had been for a time Liszt's pupil, I entered into Russian state service, remaining, nevertheless, during my whole life, though a dilettante, a great and fervent admirer of that art, and a real artist in my heart. I sign, with veneration to your person, Dr. Mason, and have the honor to remain,

Yours very truly,<br>ADOLPH STANGE.

### BERLIOZ IN WEIMAR

HECTOR BERLIOZ came to Weimar occasionally, and I remember particularly one of his visits, which took place in May,

1854. He was famous as an orchestral conductor, and I saw him in this capacity in a concert the program of which consisted exclusively of his own compositions. These were especially attractive on account of their magnificent orchestral coloring. In this regard he was certainly wonderful, and produced many gorgeous effects. His masterly skill and intelligence in the treatment and development of his themes were also everywhere apparent. Every detail received careful attention, and the result was admirable.

Not long afterward he gave a similar concert in the Leipsic Gewandhaus Hall, on which occasion the Weimar contingent was of course present. There was no need of our services as claqueurs, however, for the hall was crowded and the audience demonstrative.

Schubert was spontaneous and inspired, and thus stands in contrast to Berlioz. Melody gushed from Schubert at such a rate, and musical ideas crowded upon each other so rapidly, that he did not take time to work up his compositions. There are a few which he elaborated with care, but they are the exceptions, and emphasize the general spontaneity of his work. If he had constructive power,—and certain passages in his work show that he had,—he nevertheless failed to make adequate use of it. His music is charming and delightful on account of its melodious freshness and naïveté. It appeals directly to the heart. The only drawback is his servile adherence to conventionalities, such, for instance, as the old method of invariably repeating every section of a movement.

Beethoven stands as the model of constructive power and emotional expression in happy equipoise. Both the head and the heart are satisfactorily employed, and in his orchestral treatment they find full expression. This is true of all of his concerted works ; but his weak point is manifested in his pianoforte compositions, especially in the sonatas, which are not idiomatic of the instrument for which they were written. It is not intended to find fault with the music *per se*. It is simply to say that his ideas are all orchestrally

conceived, and as they are not in the nature of the pianoforte, that instrument is
inadequate to their true expression. The
sonatas are not pianistic, idiomatic—
*klaviermässig.* Had he written them for
orchestra, we would have had thirty-two
symphonies.

Chopin's compositions are the very es-
sence and consummation of the piano, and
he is, therefore, the pianoforte composer
*par excellence.* On the other hand, his
orchestral work is weak and incompetent,
as, for example, the accompaniment to his
concertos and some other pieces.

Schumann is at home in both directions.
He is polyphonic in orchestral treatment,
and at the same time thoroughly pianistic. Without suggesting comparisons,
his music is *musical* and complete. Beethoven's is heroic.

### ENTERTAINING LISZT'S "YOUNG BEETHOVEN"

LISZT sometimes left Weimar for a few
days in order to be present at or to conduct

music festivals. On one of these occasions, early in June, 1854, I remained alone at home on account of slight illness. As Klindworth had gone to London for concert-playing and pianoforte-teaching, I had moved into a suite of rooms in the Hotel zum Erbprinzen. As a matter of interest to pianists I here note the fact that these identical rooms had been occupied by Hummel several years previously.

On the afternoon of the day on which Liszt left with his cortège the head waiter came to me, saying that a young man who had just arrived was in the café inquiring for Liszt and seemed disappointed on learning of his absence. "I told him," said the waiter, "that you were the only one of the family here. Will you see him?" I assented, and in a few moments he ushered in a young man about twenty-four years of age, of strong features and with a great shock of dark hair, who introduced himself as Anton Rubinstein. I explained to him that Liszt had gone away for three or four days to conduct a festival, that I could not say precisely when he would return; but in the meantime, if I could make him feel at home, I should be very glad.

After some conversation he asked me to play. I remember very well how he looked sitting on the sofa, and the position of the piano in the room. I played, but he did not. I had a suspicion that he was inveigling me into playing without any intention of allowing me to take his measure. He sat there like a gruff Russian bear; or perhaps my imagination helped to produce this impression.

Rubinstein was already quite well known as a child prodigy, but of course not nearly so famous as he afterward became. I do not recollect paying him very much attention during Liszt's absence, but, then, he did not allow me—he was rambling about all the time; nor did I hear him play before Liszt came back. When Liszt returned, Rubinstein was immediately invited to take up his residence on the Altenburg. I remember that there, one afternoon, he played many of his own compositions. His playing was full of rush and fire, and characterized by strong emotional temperament. He had a big technic and reveled in dash and fire. Those who heard Mark Hambourg here during the winter of 1899–1900 can form a very good idea of Rubinstein's personal appearance at the time of which I write, and also his very pronounced style of playing. His early touch lacked the mellow and tender beauty of tone which distinguished it in later years.

### RUBINSTEIN'S OPPOSITION TO WAGNER

RUBINSTEIN'S well-known dislike of Wagner, it seems to me, was temperamental in a large degree, and it was quite natural that he was not in agreement with him. Doubtless Chopin would not have approved of Wagner's music, whatever he might have thought of his method. The melodies of Chopin and Rubinstein are full of sentiment and well defined, and their compositions run in entirely opposite channels from those of Wagner, whose music is a vast sensuous upheaval, which proceeds uninterruptedly from the beginning of an act to the end.

All musicians have a good deal of self-esteem.    Rubinstein had his own way of composing, which corresponded to his musical temperament.    He had to write everything just as it suited his musical ear, and he could not conceive of any one else having as fine a musical ear as he. At all events, he never stopped long enough to find out if any one else had. Few musicians do.    Liszt was fond of Rubinstein, and used to call him the "young Beethoven," on account of a certain fancied resemblance he bore to the great composer.    He also recognized Rubinstein's great ability as a pianist, although I think that as a player he rated Tausig much higher.    Many years after I left Weimar a relative of mine met Liszt in Rome.    She had a short time previous to this heard Rubinstein in concert, and was in a state of great enthusiasm about his playing, and so expressed herself to Liszt.    His sole comment was, "Have you ever heard Tausig?"    The inference was that those who had heard Rubinstein and not Tausig had missed hearing the greater of the two.    I think Liszt regarded Tausig as the best of all his pupils.

As I have said once before in these pages, I never saw Liszt after leaving Weimar in July, 1854.    I occasionally received letters from him—several of them quite long and exceedingly entertaining.    One of these (the original in French) is reproduced here because it is characteristic of his pleasantry and good humor :

MY DEAR MASON : Although I do not know at what stage of your brilliant artistic peregrinations these lines will reach you, I feel assured that you are not ignorant that I am very, very sincerely and affectionately obliged to you for keeping me in kind remembrance, a fact to which the musical journals which you have sent me bear good witness. The "Musical Gazette" of New York has in particular given me genuine satisfaction, not alone on account of the agreeable and flattering things concerning me personally which it contains, but furthermore because this journal seems to me to inculcate an excellent and superior direction of opinion in your country. As you know, my dear Mason, I have no other self-interest than to serve the good cause of art so far as is possible, and wherever I find men who are making conscientious efforts in the same direction, I rejoice and am strengthened by the good example which they give me. Be so good as to present to your brother, the head editor of the "Musical Review," as I suppose, my very sincere thanks and compliments. If he would like to receive some communication from Weimar upon matters of interest which occur in the musical world of Germany, I will willingly have them sent to him through the medium of Mr. Pohl, who, by the way, does not live any longer at Dresden, where the numbers of the "Musical Gazette" were addressed by mistake, but at Weimar in the Kaufstrasse. His wife, one of the best harpists that I know, stands among the virtuosos of our "Chapelle," and is an important factor in the representation of the opera, as also in concerts.

Apropos of concerts, in a few days I will send you the program of a series of symphonic performances, which ought to have been established here several years ago, and to which I consider it an honor and a duty to give definite encouragement from the year 1855.

I expect Berlioz toward the end of January. We shall then hear his trilogy "L'Enfance du

Christ," of which you already know "La Fuite
en Egypte." To this he has added two other
short oratorios, "Le Songe d'Herode" and
"L'Arrivée à Saïs."

The dramatic symphony "Faust" (in four
parts, with solos and choruses) will also be
given in full during his stay here.

In regard to visits from artists who have
been personally agreeable to me during the
last month, I would name Clara Schumann
and Litolff.

In Brendel's journal, "Neue Zeitschrift,"
you will find an article signed with my name,
on Mme. Schumann, whom I have again heard
with that sympathy and absolute admiration
which her talent compels.

As for Litolff, I confess that he has made
a very vivid impression on me. His fourth
concerto symphony (manuscript) is a very
remarkable composition, and he played it in
so masterly a manner, with such verve, with
such boldness and certainty, that I derived
intense pleasure from it.

If there was a little of the quadruped in the
amazing execution of Dreyschock (and this
comparison should not vex him; is not the
lion classed among quadrupeds as well as the
poodle?), in that of Litolff, there is certainly
something *winged;* moreover, he has all the
superiority over Dreyschock that a biped
having ideas, imagination, and sensibility has
over another biped which imagines itself

possessed of all this wealth — often very embarrassing!

Do you continue your familiar intercourse with the Old Cognac in the New World, my dear Mason? Let me again commend *measure* to you, an essential quality for musicians. In truth, I am not too well qualified to extol the *quantity* of this *quality*, for, if I remember rightly, I have often employed tempo rubato when I was giving my concerts (work which I would not begin again for anything in the world), and even quite recently I have written a long symphony in three parts, called "Faust" (without text or vocal parts), in which the *horrible* measures $\frac{7}{8}$, $\frac{7}{4}$, $\frac{5}{4}$ alternate with common time and $\frac{3}{4}$. By virtue of which I conclude that you should be satisfied with $\frac{7}{8}$ of a little bottle of old cognac in the evening, and never exceed five quarts!

Raff, in his first volume of "Wagner Frage," has thoroughly realized something like *five quarts* of doctrinal sufficiency, but that is an unadvisable example to copy in a critical matter, and above all in the matter of cognac and other spirits!

My dear Mason, excuse these bad jokes, justified only by my good intentions; that you may bear yourself valiantly, physically and morally, is the most cordial wish of

Your very friendly affectionate

F. Liszt.

Weimar, December 14, 1854.

You did not know Rubinstein in Weimar?[1]
He spent some time here, and was conspicu-
ously different from the opaque mass of self-
styled *composer-pianists* who do not even know
what it is to play the piano, still less with what
fuel it is necessary to heat one's self in order to
compose, so that with what they lack in talent
for composition they fancy themselves pianists, and vice versa.

Rubinstein will publish forthwith about fifty
compositions — concertos, trios, symphonies,
songs, light pieces, etc., which deserve notice.

Laub has left Weimar.    Ed. Singer takes his
place in our orchestra.    The latter gives much
pleasure here, and is pleased himself also.

Cornelius, Pohl, Raff, Pruckner, Schreiber,
and all the new school of the new Weimar
send you their friendliest greetings, to which
I add a hearty *shake-hand.*            F. L.

Other letters received from Liszt are
perhaps not very important, but with one
exception never having been published
before, they are printed in the Appendix.

Pupils of Liszt and Thalberg and their
pupils in search of an entertaining diver-
sion may amuse themselves by tracing

[1] As I have elsewhere stated, I was the first to meet
Rubinstein in Weimar, while Liszt was away.

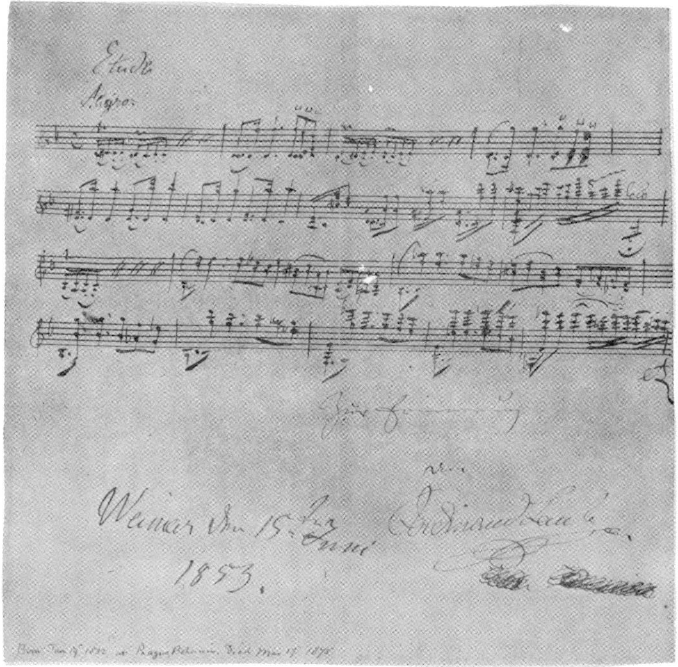

their musical pedigree back to Bach,
Mozart, and Beethoven, and thus lay claim
to very distinguished ancestry, as shown
in the following table :

Liszt, Franz, born Oct. 22, 1811.
Czerny, Carl, born Feb. 21, 1791.
Beethoven, Ludwig van, born Dec. 16, 1770.
Neefe, Christian G., born Feb. 5, 1748.
Hiller, Johann A., born Dec. 25, 1728.
Homilius, G. A., born Feb. 2, 1714.
Bach, Johann Sebastian, born March 21, 1685.
Thalberg, Sigismond, born Jan. 7, 1812.
Hummel, J. N., born Nov. 14, 1778.
Mozart, Wolfgang A., born Jan. 27, 1756.

If there be any whose pride is not
sufficiently nourished by this display, they
may go still further and show, by authentic records, a descent through Bach from
Josquin Desprez, the most eminent contrapuntist of the Netherlands school, who
lived about 1450–1521.

During the winter of 1879–80, which I
spent at Wiesbaden on account of ill
health, I received a very cordial invitation to visit Liszt at Weimar some time
in July, and made plans to do so, which

were frustrated, however, through unforeseen circumstances. Bülow, when on his first visit here, in 1875, told me that the old charm had entirely passed away. The "Golden Time" was among the things that were.

The last message I had from Liszt was brought to me by Mr. Louis Geilfuss of Steinway & Sons, who met Liszt in one of the streets of Bayreuth only a few days before his death, which occurred somewhat unexpectedly on July 31, 1886.

## AT WORK IN AMERICA

WHEN I returned from Europe in 1854 my parents had moved from Boston, and were living at Orange, New Jersey.

On landing in New York, I hurried to Boston, and went immediately to the house of Mr. Webb. This had been my constant purpose ever since the time I left America in 1849. In due course Miss Webb and I became engaged, and were married on March 12, 1857.

My first enterprise after returning from Germany was a concert tour. This I believe to have been the first exclusively pianoforte recital tour ever undertaken in this country. Gottschalk, who was here at that time, had traveled about giving concerts, but he was never without a singer or associate of some kind.

In 1853 I had attended a recital given
in Frankfort, Germany, by Ferdinand
Hiller, the program of which consisted
exclusively of his own compositions, concluding with a free improvisation on
themes suggested by the audience.  My
recitals were fashioned after this, only I
played very few of my own pieces.  The
programs were somewhat similar to those
of the present time, ranging from Beethoven and Chopin to Liszt.    At that
time Bach's name, according to my recollection, was never seen on a pianoforte-
recital program.  A large number of these
compositions, such as  Liszt's "Twelfth
Rhapsody" and Chopin's "Fantasie Im-
promptu," were played for the first time
in this country at these concerts.


## TOURING THE COUNTRY

My friend Oliver Dyer managed the tour.
My brothers Daniel and Lowell were at
this time booksellers and publishers in
New York, under the firm-name of Mason
Brothers, and Mr. Dyer was connected

with them in business.    He was a man of
action, and possessed good literary ability.
He had lived for a time in Washington as
reporter of speeches made in Congress,
and later on he was connected with Robert
Bonner on the "Ledger."

He arranged a pamphlet in which he
set forth and doubtless embellished the
facts connected with my sojourn in Germany and the favor with which my playing had been received.    When, in the
course of our tour, we arrived at a town
where a lecture was to be given,—not an
uncommon  occurrence,—he would take
down the lecture stenographically and
write notices of it for the local papers.
The editors appreciated this favor, and
were so kindly disposed toward us that
they would print any advance notices he
chose to write about me.    In what he
wrote of me, however, I was not willing to
have him go to extremes, though he would
frequently slip something into the paper
without my knowledge, leaving me to
find fault with him the next day.

All along the route it was difficult to

persuade people that an entertainment of pianoforte-playing exclusively could be made interesting. They had never heard of such a thing, and insisted that there ought to be some singing for the sake of variety. We stopped in Albany, Troy, Utica, and many other places on the way to Chicago, where I gave two concerts, one of which took place on New Year's eve. After the concert I attended a large reception given in a private residence. I remember being struck by the fact, as it seemed to me, that there were so many young ladies at this reception, and I asked the hostess if there were no married ladies in Chicago. "Why, Mr. Mason," she replied, "there are only two or three unmarried ladies in the room." At that period Chicago was full of young men who had come from the Eastern States, principally New England. After staying in Chicago for two or three years and getting well started in business they would get married, many of them going to their native places for their brides. This accounted for the youthful appearance of the assemblage, and illustrates in part the very rapid growth of Chicago.

Up to the time we arrived in Chicago we had rainy weather constantly, and partly on this account we were out of pocket. Dyer was for going back to New York by the quickest route. I said : "No ; I am going back through the same towns, and shall give concerts in every one of them. If the people liked my playing well enough they will come again and bring their neighbors. If they did not like it, I shall soon find it out." As it turned out, I had much larger audiences all the way home.

### "YANKEE DOODLE" AND "OLD HUNDRED"

COPYING the custom of Ferdinand Hiller, I used to close my concerts by an improvisation upon themes suggested by the audience. All sorts of themes were put into the hat—from Mozart, Beethoven, "Jordan is a hard road to travel," "We won't go home till morning," and many negro melodies. I had a faculty of developing a subject in such a way as to hold my audience.

One night somebody sent up the request that I should play simultaneously "Old Hundred" with one hand and "Yankee Doodle" with the other. This I did, merely to show that even two such dissimilar melodies could be played together in a musical way. There was a good deal of applause, but also considerable hissing from the religious element, so I made a speech explaining that I meant no disrespect to "Old Hundred" by placing it in such close connection with "Yankee Doodle," and that the melody which had to a certain extent been adopted as a national air was on that account worthy of being played with any hymn.

Fifteen years later, in 1870, George F. Root, who had assisted my father in his musical convention work in the East, but who had settled in Chicago and was doing the same kind of pioneer work in the West, was holding a summer musical convention in South Bend, Indiana. He wished to introduce piano as well as vocal teaching, and invited me to take charge of the piano classes. It was a fearfully hot summer, and during the month I was in South Bend the temperature was continuously close to 100°. Toward the close of the season concerts were given, and it was so hot that in lieu of a dress-coat I wore a linen duster, cut off at the waist.

At the last concert I received a request from two or three people to play "Yankee Doodle" with one hand and "Old Hundred" with the other. Possibly they had heard me do so in 1855. Remembering my experience then, I made a few remarks, in which I told them that some little feeling had been created fifteen years before by my doing the same thing, but that—and here I got a little mixed—in playing "Yankee Doodle" with "Old Hundred" I did not intend any disrespect to "Yankee Doodle." At this the audience began to laugh. Schuyler Colfax, who was then Vice-President of the United States, was on the stage behind me, and I could hear him chuckling. I thought to myself, "Well, I have made some funny mistake, though I don't know what it is, so I won't go back and try to correct it."

Afterward Mr. Colfax, who was a noted speaker, told me that whenever he made a *lapsus linguae*, if it amused the audience he never attempted to correct it.

On my return from this concert tour to New York, I established the series of chamber-music concerts which, begun as an experiment, continued thirteen years. I also settled down as a teacher. While I had returned from Weimar with the full intention of continuing my career as a piano-virtuoso, and while my concert tour had been promising enough, I found that the public demanded a constant repetition of pieces to which it happened to take a liking, and I knew that I should soon weary of playing the same things over and over again. Moreover, I felt that from my father I had inherited a certain capacity for giving instruction, and that the chamber-music concerts and engagements with the Philharmonic and at other concerts in New York and elsewhere would serve to keep up my practice as a virtuoso.

### SETTLING DOWN TO TEACH

In 1855 I accepted as pupils some four or five young ladies who were being educated at a fashionable boarding-school in New York. One of these girls was very bright and intelligent but without special musical talent. She was extremely averse to application in study, and the problem for me was to invent some way by which mental concentration could be compelled, for from the moment she sat down to the piano to practise she was constantly looking at the clock to see if her practice-hour was up. After a little study I found that in playing a scale up one octave and back, without intermission, in ⅜ time, there are necessarily nine repetitions of the scale before the initial tone falls again on the first part of the measure. Thus,

and so on until another accent falls upon the initial C. Such an exercise is called

a rhythmus, and the repetitions compel
mental concentration just as surely as
the addition of a column of figures does.
I found that if the compass was extended
four octaves, thus, from

the nine repetitions of the scale would
require from three to four minutes if
played at a moderate rate of speed.   I
saw at once that a state of mental concentration could not be avoided by the
pupil, and that in this exercise lay a basic
principle.   I gave the exercise to my
pupil.    The result was that when the
next lesson-hour came around and I asked
her how she found the new exercise, she
exclaimed : "How do I like it?   Why,
you have played a pretty trick on me !
It took me nearly an hour to accomplish
it ; but I like it.   Why did you not give
it to me before?"   "Because," I said, "I
invented it simply in order to compel
your attention to your work."   Following
up the principle of grouping the tones, I

found there was apparently no end to the possible varieties. Two or three years after I had published a system of instruction based upon this principle I came across a statement in the writings of Moscheles to the effect that some one would eventually apply rhythmic forms to all sorts of finger-exercises, and that this was a very desirable thing to bring about. It was precisely the means by which I had first taught my boarding-school pupil how to concentrate her mind upon her practice.

The idea of starting a series of matinées of chamber-music occurred to me. I wished especially to introduce to the public the "Grand Trio in B Major, Op. 8," by Johannes Brahms, and to play other concerted works, both classical and modern, for this kind of work interested me more than mere piano-playing. So I asked Carl Bergmann, who was the most noted orchestral conductor of those days, and thus well acquainted with musicians, to get together a good string quartet. This he accomplished in a day or two, and

made me acquainted with Theodore
Thomas, first violin; Joseph Mosenthal,
second violin; and George Matzka, viola,
Bergmann himself being the violoncellist.
We very soon began rehearsing, and our
first concert, or rather matinée, took
place in Dodworth's Hall, opposite Elev-
enth street, and one door above Grace
Church in Broadway. The program was
as follows:

Tuesday, November 27, 1855

1. Quartet in D Minor, Strings .   *Schubert*
2. Romance from Tannhäuser,
    "Abendstern" . . . . .   *Wagner*
3. Pianoforte Solo, Fantasie Im-
    promptu, Op. 66 (first time)   *Chopin*
    [Deux Préludes, D flat and G,
    Op. 24 . . . . . . . . .   *Heller*
4. Variations Concertante for
    Violoncello and Piano, Op. 17. *Mendelssohn*
5. "Feldwärts flog ein Vöglein"   *Nicolai*
6. Grand Trio in B Major, Op. 8,
    Piano, Violin, and Cello (first
    time) . . . . . . . . .   *Brahms*

It will be observed that we started out
with a novelty, Brahms's Trio, which was
played then for the first time in America.

I repeated it in Boston a few weeks later
with the assistance of some members of
the Mendelssohn Quintet Club. It received appreciation on both occasions and
was listened to attentively, but without
enthusiasm. The newspapers spoke well
of it in general, but there were some who
regarded it as constrained and unnatural.
The vocal pieces were inserted in deference to the prevailing idea of the period
that no musical entertainment could be
enjoyed by the public without some singing. We quickly got over that notion,
and thenceforth, with rare exceptions, our
programs were confined to instrumental
music.

It was my purpose in organizing these
concerts to make a point of producing
chamber-work, which had never before
been heard here, especially those of Schumann and other modern writers.


THEODORE THOMAS AT TWENTY

THE organization as originally formed
would probably have remained intact dur-

ing all the years the concerts lasted had it not become apparent almost from the start that Theodore Thomas had in him the genius of conductorship. He possessed by nature a thoroughly musical organization and was a born conductor and leader.

Before we had been long together it became apparent that there was more or less friction between Thomas and Bergmann, who, being the conductor of the Germania and afterward of the Philharmonic orchestras, also a player of long experience and the organizer of the quartet, naturally assumed the leadership in the beginning. The result was that Bergmann withdrew after the first year, and Bergner, a fine violoncellist and active member of the Philharmonic Society, took his place. The organization was then called the Mason and Thomas Quartet, and so styled it won a wide reputation throughout the country. I should say in passing that Bergmann was an excellent though not a great conductor.

From the time that Thomas took the

MATZKA    MOSENTHAL    BERGNER    THOMAS    MASON

THE MASON-THOMAS QUARTET

leadership free and untrammeled, the quartet improved rapidly. His dominating influence was felt and acknowledged by us all. Moreover, he rapidly developed a talent for making programs by putting pieces into the right order of sequence, thus avoiding incongruities. He brought this art to perfection in the arrangement of his symphony concert programs.

Our viola, Matzka, was also an excellent musician, and for many years the first viola of the Philharmonic orchestra. Mosenthal, who played second violin, achieved a wide reputation as composer and conductor, in which latter capacity he did splendid work for the Mendelssohn Glee Club. He was also one of the best teachers of piano and violin in New York.

### THOMAS AS CONDUCTOR

THOMAS'S fame as a conductor has entirely overshadowed his earlier reputation as a violinist. He had a large tone, the tone of a player of the highest rank. He lacked the perfect finish of a great violinist, but he played in a large, quiet, and reposeful manner. This seemed to pass from his violin-playing into his conducting, in which there is the same sense of largeness and dignity, coupled, however, with the artistic finish which he lacked as a violinist. He is a very great conductor, the greatest we have ever had here, not only in the Beethoven symphonies and other classical music, but in Liszt, Wagner, and the extreme moderns. Why should he not conduct Wagner as well as anybody else, or better? Everything is large about Wagner, and everything is large about Thomas. His rates of tempo are in accord with those of the most celebrated conductors whom I heard fifty years ago. In modern times the tendency has been toward an increased rate of speed, and this detracts in large measure from the impressiveness of the works, especially those of Mozart, Beethoven, Von Weber, and others.

That the skilful orchestral conductor does not rely solely upon the ear but sometimes receives assistance from the eye in his work is illustrated by an experience of Theodore Thomas which he related while dining at my house some two years since.    On one occasion, when a benefit concert was tendered to him, the orchestra was increased to jubilee dimensions, and I think there were sixteen violoncello-players, with other instruments in due proportion.    During the final rehearsal Mr. Thomas became aware of some imper-fections, probably of phrasing, and traced the error to the violoncellists, but could not at first detect the individual whose fault it was.    On closer scrutiny he ob-served that one of them was bowing in the wrong way, and thus obscuring the phrasing.

The newspapers, in reviewing the con-cert, mentioned this incident as illus-trating the wonderfully sensitive ear of the conductor, whereas on this occa-sion, at least, the eye was the detective agent.

It is possible, however, for a trained ear to detect errors in mere manipulation,

and I am reminded by one of my former
pupils that, having taken advantage, during one of his lessons, of my momentary
absence in an adjoining room, to play a
passage according to his own ideas of
proper technic, he was astonished to hear
me call out to him that he had used
the wrong finger in striking one of the
keys.

That Thomas had entire confidence in
himself was shown in the outset of his
career.   One evening, as he came home
tired out from his work, and after dinner
had settled himself in a comfortable place
for a good rest, a message came to him
from the Academy of Music, about two
blocks away from his house in East
Twelfth street.   An opera season was in
progress there, and, what was not unusual,
the management was in financial difficulties.   Anschütz, who was conductor of
the orchestra, had refused to take the
desk unless paid what was due him.   The
orchestra was in its place, the audience
was seated, but there was no conductor.
Would Thomas come to the rescue?   He

THEODORE THOMAS
ABOUT TWENTY-FOUR YEARS OLD

had never conducted opera, and the work for the evening's performance was an opera with which he was unfamiliar. Here was a life's opportunity, and Thomas was equal to the occasion. He thought for a moment, then said, "I will." He rose quickly, got himself into his dress-suit, hurried to the Academy of Music, and conducted the opera as if it were a common experience. He was not a man to say, "Give me time until next week." He was always ready for every opportunity.

On Christmas day, 1900, a friend presented me with a calendar for the year 1901. It has a leaf for each day of the year. The calendar evidently required much labor in preparation, and necessitated correspondence with many friends at home as well as abroad, and many are the cordial responses that were received. The result is a daily pleasure and surprise. The leaf for February 11, 1901, the day of my present writing, has reference to the third concert of chamber-music, eighth season of Mason and Thomas, which took place on Tuesday evening, February 10, 1862 :

Tuesday, February 10, 1862

The third soirée of Mason and Thomas had the following program :

| | |
|---|---|
| Quartet, C Major, No. 2 . . . . | *Cherubini* |
| Piano Trio, D Major, Op. 70, No. 1 | *Beethoven* |
| Quartet, A Major, Op. 41, No. 3 . | *Schumann* |

A program as interesting and fresh to-day as thirty-eight years ago. The weather was very cold,— below zero,— and during the largo of the trio the gas gave out. We continued playing for some time, but finally had to stop. The " Geister " [the composition here referred to is called by the Germans the "Geister Trio"] did not assist us ! Do you remember the fact?

Es ist schon lange her.

THEODORE THOMAS.

KARL KLAUSER, MUSICAL DIRECTOR<br>AT MISS PORTER'S SCHOOL

THROUGH Mosenthal our quartet became acquainted with Mr. Karl Klauser, who was an active and enthusiastic musician of thorough education, and who has accomplished a great deal of useful work both as a compiler and teacher of classic and modern compositions. Mr. Klauser is a native of St. Petersburg, born of German parents; he came to New York in 1850, and was engaged as musical director in Miss Porter's famous school for young ladies in 1855, a post which he filled with credit and ability for many years. He was enthusiastically fond of chamber-music, and frequently attended the rehearsals of our quartet; and it was through him that we were induced to give recitals in Farmington six months after our beginning in New York. On Thursday, June 26, 1856, our program was as follows:

String Quartet in E flat, No. 4 . .     *Mozart*
Trio, Piano, Violin, and Violoncello,
  G Minor, Op. 15, No. 2 . . . . *Rubinstein*
Variations from Quartet No. 5 . . *Beethoven*
Also solos for pianoforte and for violoncello.

On the following day another recital was given, with an entire change of program.

At that time one of the undergraduates

of the school was a young girl who is now
the wife of a distinguished lawyer of New
York, and is herself prominent in good
works. Not long ago I received from her
the following very agreeable letter about
the early Farmington days:

MY DEAR DR. MASON: I am glad to hear
that you are to share your pleasant "Memories" with your friends. I hope, in looking
back to the happy times when you were
young, you will not forget your annual visits
to dear old Farmington; for if you do not
remember them in words, many old admirers
will wonder how you could fail to make much
of occasions so precious to them.

As one of Miss Porter's girls, who can now
live over again the coming to town of William
Mason, Theodore Thomas, J. Mosenthal, G.
Matzka, F. Bergner, and the long-looked-for
chamber-concerts, I feel sure that in all of
your generous giving of a God-given genius,
you never gave more real pleasure than you
gave those school-girls and teachers hungry
for a taste of life outside the school, and for
good music, the best of all company. You
were then to them what you only hoped to be
after years of hard work,— great men in your
profession,— and they could not have dressed
with more care or been more excited if they

had been going to listen with royalty to the greatest of the old masters.

Among the choicest of my pictures of Farmington days is that of the girls in white and dainty pinks and greens and blues, with flowers to wear and flowers to throw to you, almost dancing down that beautiful street on a summer day to "the concert," and in the foreground a quaint dark figure whom all the girls remember on festive occasions as bearing the burden of her choice with a New England sense of propriety at war with her keen sympathy with all that is natural in young people, and with the pride in her good-looking family which made her blind to their youthful follies. That was long ago when we were giddy girls, but the verdict of our heads and hearts was a true one.

Sure that your memories, dear Dr. Mason, must be bright in the sunlight of so many warm friendships, I am listening to the music of long ago.

March 31, 1901.

### LOUIS MOREAU GOTTSCHALK

I KNEW Gottschalk well, and was fascinated by his playing, which was full of brilliancy and bravura. His strong, rhythmic accent, his vigor and dash, were excit-

ing and always aroused enthusiasm. He
was the perfection of his school, and his
effects had the sparkle and effervescence
of champagne. He was as far as possible
from being an interpreter of chamber or
classical music, but, notwithstanding this,
some of the best musicians of the strict
style were frequently to be seen among
his audience, among others Carl Bergmann, who told me that he always heard
Gottschalk with intense enjoyment. He
first made his mark through his arrangement of creole melodies. They were well
defined rhythmically, and he played them
with absolute rhythmic accuracy. This
clear definition in his interpretation contributed more than anything else to the
fascination which he always exerted over
his audience. He did not care for the
German school, and on one occasion, after
hearing me play Schumann at one of the
Mason-Thomas matinées, he said : "Mason,
I do not understand why you spend so
much of your time over music like that ;
it is stiff and labored, lacks melody, spontaneity, and naïveté. It will eventually

vitiate your musical taste and bring you into an abnormal state."

Although an enthusiastic admirer of Beethoven symphonies and other orchestral works, he did not care for the pianoforte sonatas, which he said were not written in accordance with the nature of the instrument. It has been said that he could play all of the sonatas by heart; but I am quite sure that Mr. Richard Hoffman, who was his intimate friend, will sustain me in the assertion that such was not the fact.

I have known Mr. Hoffman for more than fifty years, having met him for the first time in the year 1847 or thereabout. His playing is still characterized by precision, accuracy, and clearness in phrasing, with an excellent technic, combined with repose. I have many times enjoyed his artistic interpretations, and I heard him with great pleasure not a long while ago, on the occasion of his fiftieth anniversary as a teacher in this country.

Returning to Gottschalk, a funny thing

happened one day.   At the time of which
I write, forty-five years ago, William
Hall & Sons' music-store was in Broadway, corner of Park Place, and was a
place of rendezvous for musicians.   Going
there one day, I met Gottschalk, who,
holding up the proof-sheet of a title-page
which he had just received from the
printer, said : "Read that !"    What I
read was, "The Latest Hops," in big block
letters after the fashion of an outside
music title-page.    "What    does    this
mean ?"  I  asked.   "Well,"  he  replied,
"it ought to be 'The Last Hope,' but the
printer, either by way of joke or from
stupidity, has expressed it in this way.
There is to be a new edition of my 'Last
Hope,' and I am revising it for that purpose."

I have in my autograph-book a letter
of his, undated, but written in the late
fifties :

My dear M.: If you have nothing to do,
come and spend the evening with me on Sunday next.  No formality.  Smoking required,
impropriety allowed,  and complete liberty,

My dear M..

If you have nothing
to do come & spend the evening
with me on Sunday next. No
formality. Smoking required
impropriety allowed &
complete Liberty with as
little music possible. I was
going to mention that we
will have a glass of wine
& chicken salad.

Your friend

[signature]
149 E. 9th

with as little music as possible. I was going
to mention that we will have a glass of wine
and chicken salad.

                    Your friend,
                            GOTTSCHALK.
149 East Ninth Street.


PROPAGANDA FOR SCHUMANN'S MUSIC

GOTTSCHALK'S remark about my liking
for Schumann's music was at that time
echoed by others, for when I returned
from Germany and found Schumann virtually unknown here, I made it my mission to introduce his music into this
country—a labor of love in which I was
afterward greatly aided by the quartet
concerts and by my teaching. Shortly
after my return from Germany I went
to Breusing's, then one of the principal
music-stores in the city,—the Schirmers
are his successors,—and asking for certain compositions by Schumann, I was in-
formed that they had his music in stock,
but as there was no demand for it, it was
packed away in a bundle and kept in the
basement. Pretty soon, however, my pu-

pils began calling for Schumann's pieces,
and Schumann moved up from the cellar
to the main floor.   His music was expen-
sive, because it was published in sets, and
if a pupil wanted to buy one of the
"Novellettes" or "Kinderscenen," it was
necessary to purchase the whole collection.
After a while, however, some of the
music-dealers began to publish a number
of the pieces separately.   This had the
effect in some measure of opening up the
sale of his music to pupils and amateurs.

### SIGISMOND THALBERG

THALBERG'S playing was characterized by
grace, elegance, and perfection of finish in
detail.   His style was suave, courteous,
and aristocratic.   Being a pupil of Hummel, who had in turn taken lessons of
Mozart for two years, it was quite within
the line of descent that he should have
acquired the extremely smooth legato
touch of those masters.   As distinguished
from any pianist-composer up to his time,
his specialty was the surrounding of a

melody with arabesques and ornamental passages of scales and arpeggios played with rapidity, clearness, and brilliancy. Parish Alvars, the harpist, had originated this device, and Thalberg adapted it to the pianoforte, for which instrument it was better suited and more effective than on the harp.

The important influence of the upper-arm muscles in the production of powerful and resonant tones seems to have been but little known in those days.   Leopold de Meyer's constant use of these, as noted elsewhere, was apparently unconscious and instinctive.

Thalberg's octave-playing was not altogether elastic and free from rigidity, for in long-continued and rapid octave passages a close observer would have noticed a contraction of his facial muscles and a compression of the lips, which would have been avoided under the conditions of properly devitalized upper-arm muscles and loose wrists.

Shortly after his arrival in our country he went by invitation to my brother's house in West Orange, New Jersey, on a visit of some weeks. This afforded an opportunity which was not neglected, and as a result I became well acquainted with him and his method of practice. In this way he was virtually one of my best teachers, although no regular lessons were received from him. Moreover, in several of his concerts I played with him his duo for two pianofortes on themes from "Norma," and these were occasions of great artistic profit. One learned much, also, from hearing him practise. His daily exercises included scale and arpeggio passages played at various rates of speed and with different degrees of dynamic force. These were always put into rhythmic form, and the measures, sometimes in triple and sometimes in quadruple time in many varieties, were invariably indicated by means of accentuation. Dynamic effects, such as crescendos and diminuendos, also received due attention. In short, as it seems to me, he made it a point—as well in the cultivation and development of physical technic

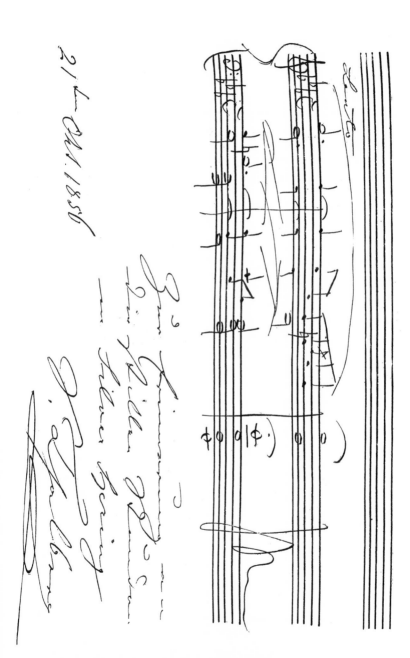

as in his public performances—to play *musically* at all times.

Thalberg's technic seemed to be confined mainly to the finger, hand, wrist, and lower-arm muscles, but these he used in such a deft manner as to draw from his instrument the loveliest tones. He was altogether opposed to the high-raised finger of some of the modern schools, and in his work entitled "L'Art du Chant applique au Piano" he cautions students against this habit. The same advice had been previously given by Carl Czerny in his "Letters on the Art of Playing the Pianoforte," namely : "Do not strike the keys from too great a height, as in this case a thud will accompany the tone."

Thalberg adds : "Gewöhnlich arbeitet man zu viel mit den Fingern und zu wenig mit dem Geiste" ("Generally one works too much with the fingers and too little with the intelligence").

This is reasonable advice, for a touch which starts off simply for strength and mechanical development, separate from other traits, becomes eventually so obstinately fixed and determined that its influence will dominate and stand constantly in the way of poetic and musical development. In this connection it is well to remember and apply the proverb: "An ounce of prevention is worth a pound of cure."

He was very fond of his grand pianofortes, both of which were made by Érard of Paris. One of these instruments was drawn upon a much larger scale than had previously been made by this or, so far as I know, by any other manufacturer. The tone was powerful and of a lovely musical character. Thalberg's idea was that the better the instrument the greater the advantage afforded the virtuoso, not only for public playing, but as well for the purpose of practice and musical development. I remember his telling me that a fine instrument even suggested ideas to the composer and furthered his work. An experience of many years has proved to me the soundness of his theory and the importance of its practical application.

The not uncommon assertion that "any piano will do for a beginner" is wrong in

principle.    How absurd to assert that any
associates will do for children in the beginning !    It is just at this tender age when
impressions are so easily received that the
best musical advantages should be afforded.
What can be better adapted to the cultivation of a musical ear than the constant
presence of musical tones of the highest
quality and purity ?    The ear requires
close musical companionship in order to
promote corresponding development.

The cultivation of a physical technic is
important, indeed indispensable, but it
should not precede or be separated from
musical companionship.  Its development
should at all stages be surrounded by a
musical atmosphere in which its adapta-
bility to the expression of poetical ideas
may be developed.    The heart and head
should be closely united.

### PEDAL AND PEDAL SIGNS—WHY NOT DISPENSE WITH THE LATTER ?

PROLONGED or organ tones are not possible on the pianoforte.  From the moment

the hammer strikes the string the tone begins to diminish in volume and soon fades away. One of the chief arts of the pianist is to sustain a tone throughout the full value of the note which represents it, and this is accomplished either by steady pressure on the key or by the use of the open pedal, frequently misnamed the loud pedal. The use of the word "loud" in this connection is illogical and misleading. The word "open" is much better, because this pedal, when pressed, causes the dampers to be raised from the strings, thus leaving them open, and so prolonging the tones. Furthermore, the open pedal is constantly used in the softest and most delicate passages. Its mission is simply to prolong the tones, whether loud or soft. In either case the tone dies rapidly away, and the pianist, sensitively aware of this, and feeling the necessity of keeping up the volume of sound, is led unconsciously to anticipate or take the next tone a little before its due time. The effect of this process in continuation is to produce a feeling of unrest on the-part of the hearer, and is fatal to repose. On this account Thalberg earnestly recommends to piano-students that "the tones invariably be held throughout their absolute or exact value" (see "L'Art du Chant"). Tones can be sustained, so far as this is possible on the pianoforte, in two ways, namely, by means of the open pedal or by holding down the keys firmly during the exact value represented by the notes. How can this value be determined? Solely through the medium of the ear. "The proof of the pudding is in the eating." The proof of musical sounds, as to quality and duration, is in the listening.

This being granted, it seems to follow that all signs, such as "Ped.," *, or √ √, etc., should be discarded as being even worse than useless, for when pupils pay careful attention to them they are apt to be guided solely by the eye. They press down the pedal at the sign "Ped.," and release it at the following asterisk (*), doing this in a merely perfunctory way, and hence they either fail to produce a true legato effect or err in the opposite direction of an over-legato, which results in a confusion of sounds. This may be best avoided by practising on an instrument of fine musical quality and beautiful singing tone, which promotes the habit of listening attentively, and thus contributes in the highest degree to the development and training of the ear.

It is true that musical temperament is inborn, and those who possess it have native insight, and hence develop with rapidity. There are, however, very many who are not "to the manner born." Such are obliged to acquire habits through persistent and persevering effort. All travel the same road, but the genius flies while the less gifted plods along. However, for the benefit and consolation of the latter, I remind them that the tortoise left the hare asleep and won the race. The ear should be cultivated for music, the eye for painting, the mind in both; and the heart especially in music, because the latter is the "language of the emotions."

A little pedal study from my work entitled "Touch and Technic" (Part IV, page 18), will serve to illustrate what I mean. It is on an elementary plane and

# PEDAL STUDY FOR THE PIANOFORTE

(*To be played throughout with one finger*)

can easily be accomplished by a beginner with a little care and ordinary perseverance.

It is to be played with only one finger, and the tones of the melody must receive special emphasis so as to stand out clearly, and they must be sustained by means of the open pedal throughout the exact length of time represented by the notes. The crescendo and diminuendo must be observed according to direction, and as a help to this effect the soft pedal may be used simultaneously, either all of the time or occasionally, in an experimental way and according to fancy. This promotes the faculty of judgment and leads to individuality, a very desirable result.

The melody is on the middle line and the accompaniment on the outer lines. The melody must predominate in power, and must be sustained throughout the exact value of its representative notes, which are mostly dotted halves, viz. : ♩. This is accomplished by firmly pressing the open pedal, the finger in the meanwhile playing the accompaniment. Thus

the tone is sustained solely by means of
the pedal.    Carefully observe the effects
of crescendo ⟨ and diminuendo ⟩.
Play strictly in time.

In the final measure still continue the
pedal pressure after the C in the treble
has been played.   There are now four
tones sounding together.   Now replace
the finger silently and without striking on
the melody key E.   While still pressing
this key raise the foot from the pedal.
This leaves the E sounding alone.   Hold
down the key until the tone has quite died
away.

### RUBINSTEIN AND THE AUTOGRAPH-HUNTER

ONE afternoon I accompanied Rubinstein
from his hotel to Steinway Hall, where he
was to give a recital.   Just outside of the
stage-entrance were two young ladies, one
of whom stepped forward and, handing
me a sheet of paper and a pencil, begged
me to ask Rubinstein for his autograph,
and to leave it for her in the dressing-

room, so that she could get it after the recital. I told her that Rubinstein did not like writing autographs; that he was a man of kindly disposition, but sometimes acted from impulse; nevertheless, I would see what could be done. So, following Rubinstein up-stairs to the retiring-room, I handed him the writing-materials, stating the young lady's request.

He took them, saying nothing, but walked with an air of determination to the window, opened it, and threw them into the street. "Mason," he said, "I don't like your country. People pry too much into private affairs." He then went on to speak of newspaper writers who had interviewed him and ingeniously beguiled him into speaking of many things which concerned solely his own personality, and the next day published all of these things in detail. He said : "There is absolutely no privacy in this country." "Rubinstein," I said, "I can quite appreciate your position, and understand why you should have come to such conclusions, but

I am sure that upon due reflection you will realize that you are doing us an injustice. You have been incessantly occupied during your sojourn here, have hurried from place to place, given concerts with hardly any intermission, and naturally have had no time to see people in their homes. You have not been able to judge of our domestic life or to mingle in society and study our habits." He admitted this at once and made due acknowledgment. Wieniawski, who was once with us when a similar conversation occurred just before the close of their stay here, said : "Mason, I regret extremely that I have not been able to go out to Orange to visit you. We have traveled constantly and rushed from place to place in order to fulfil concert engagements, so that there has been no time for social intercourse. I don't wish you to gather from my apparent neglect an idea that Poles are unsociable ; on the contrary, I assure you we are very fond of social life."

Rubinstein came here with a great reputation, and achieved a good success. He

had transcendent ability, accompanied,
however, by certain limitations.  By nature impulsive and excitable, he often lost
self-control, and in consequence he frequently anticipated his climax.  He was
like a general who excelled in a brilliant
sortie, but who had not the dogged per-
sistence necessary to a long-sustained
battle, and at the critical points he was
constantly losing his self-poise.  When,
however, he did effect a climax, it was
apt to be a great one, a jubilee.  Liszt, on
the other hand, was remarkable for his
reserve force and for the discretion with
which he made use of it ; for if, perchance,
he missed a climax he immediately made
preparation for a new one, and was always sure to reach the zenith at precisely
the right moment.

There were occasions on which Rubinstein played with the most wonderful repose, and at such times his playing was
musical and poetic in the highest degree.
This was particularly the case in slow or
moderate movements characterized by
tenderness, affection, and fervor.   But in

the rapid and spirited movements his
tendency was to run away and finally to
lose self-possession—an affliction to which
the large majority of concert-pianists are
subject.   Violinists and singers are not
nearly so much so, because they can prolong their tones with steady force, or
diminish and increase the tone at will.
As I have already pointed out, the case is
different with the pianist, for after the
piano-key has been struck the tone immediately begins to decrease in power, and
this incites the player to produce another
tone ; so he proceeds a little too quickly,
constantly gaining a little in speed and
crowding one tone upon the other.   The
effect is exasperating to the listener, who
becomes more and more restless, until
finally all quiet and repose is utterly lost.

The unevenness in Rubinstein's playing I believe to have been wholly due to
the temperamental moods of a man of
extreme artistic sensitiveness.   He was
a thoroughly conscientious artist and
worked at the piano incessantly many
hours a day.   I remember his once saying

to me : "I dislike nothing more than to have people say to me, as they frequently do, 'But you do not have to practise, for you are a born genius and get everything by nature.' It is provoking to listen to such stuff after having worked so hard."

### EVOLUTION IN MUSICAL IDEAS
### BEETHOVEN PIANOFORTE RECITALS

No pianist ever dreamed of playing Beethoven's sonatas in public in those days. They were reserved for the parlor ; and one, or two at most, were enough for an evening. The mental absorption of this amount was sufficient. Lighter pieces filled out the program. I am quite sure that it was Bülow who first played several of Beethoven's sonatas consecutively at a recital. I learned of this through Anton Rubinstein when he was here in 1873. He spoke of it as being an extraordinary thing, and added that, as a musician, he could not give it his approval. It might be a scientific thing to do, but was certainly not congenial to a true musical nature, which required variety. A dinner consisting of heavy dishes throughout, without the interspersion of condiments, vegetables, and tarts to stir and incite the appetite, would be both distasteful and fatal to good digestion. The pieces selected for the musical feast should be homogeneously arranged ; and so should the various courses of the dinner.

However, notwithstanding what Rubinstein said in 1873, I noticed that, but a comparatively short time afterward, he also began the practice of giving recitals at which he played several sonatas in sequence. It is possible that he did this less to gratify his own personal artistic tastes than in deference to those of the public who had not his musical organization, and so could stand the intensity of the thing while he profited by the physical practice.

## RUBINSTEIN'S FAVORITE SEAT AT A PIANOFORTE RECITAL

RUBINSTEIN, as a listener, was particular as to the location of his seat at a concert or recital of pianoforte music, and always sought a place in one of the galleries on the left hand, facing the stage. Thus he sat in the corner diagonal to the pianoforte, looking over the right shoulder of the player.

It is true that even on the ground floor or parterre of a hall this position affords a great advantage, and the tones of the pianoforte are essentially more full of resonance and musical tone than in any other location. This may be accounted for on the theory that the raised lid of the instrument deflects the sound in that direction. There is a corresponding disadvantage in a position on the opposite side of the house, especially if seated on the ground floor near the stage. I have frequently tried both of these positions, and always with the same result; hence I have learned to make due allowance in judging of the pianist. A listener unaware of this difference may seriously err in estimating the tone quality of the instrument.

BACH'S "TRIPLE CONCERTO" AND
"LES AGRÉMENTS"

In Bach's time many embellishments were
used in playing the clavichord.    They
were all included under the general title
*Les Agréments*, or, in German, *Manieren*.
Of these the mordent, almost identical
with the modern *Pralltriller*, was in most
frequent use.    It is quite a little thing
and simple enough, but there are few
players who succeed in giving it the right
snap or rattle, without which its true
significance is wholly lost.    I have already
mentioned playing this concerto with
Klindworth and Pruckner at a court concert in Weimar.    While previously rehearsing it, Liszt was very particular in
his directions, especially regarding the
mordents, and we did our best to follow
them.    Moreover, Liszt was an authority.
He always made thorough investigation
of a subject before expressing an opinion
upon it, and he was very careful to give a
historically accurate and truthful rendering of these old-fashioned ornaments.    I

afterward found that when three pianists came together for the purpose of playing this concerto a good deal of time was wasted in discussing the proper way of playing the mordent.   It was on the program of the Mason-Thomas matinées in New York more than once, and on one occasion we had the assistance of the well-known pianists Messrs. Timm and Scharfenberg.   There was no friction at that time, as the three performers were of one mind.

In May, 1873, Theodore Thomas arranged a grand musical festival in New York, of which Rubinstein was the principal attraction.   The "Triple Concerto" was one of the features of the festival. Rubinstein played the first piano, and Mills and I the other two.

The concerto has the accompaniment of a string quartet, which may be doubled or increased to the size of a small orchestra if desired.   It was thought best to have a preliminary rehearsal for the three pianos alone, and a time was appointed for our meeting together at my studio in

Steinway Hall.   Mr. Thomas, not being
familiar with the concerto, wished to be
present in order to become acquainted
with it, and at the appointed time was the
first to make his appearance.   I told him
that Rubinstein, not precise in historical
methods, would play the mordents in accordance with the mood in which he
happened to be.   "However," I continued, "I have an old book by Friedrich
Wilhelm Marpurg, published in Berlin in
1765, in which he gives written examples
of all of the *Manieren*.   We will show
this to Rubinstein and have some fun.
But I do not propose to waste time in
discussions.   He can play as he likes, and
Mills and I will follow suit."

Rubinstein shortly made his appearance, and Mills came a little later.   I told
Rubinstein about my ancient authority,
adding that we should be spared the tedi-
ousness of a discussion as to the manner
of playing.   "Let me see the old book,"
said Rubinstein.   Running over the
leaves, he came to the illustrations of the
mordent.   The moment his eyes fell upon

them he exclaimed : "All wrong ; here is the way I play it," and going to the piano, he played as follows :

This is what Marpurg calls a kind of double mordent, or *Doppelschlag*. The three keys are struck almost simultaneously, but the middle one only is held down, while the upper and lower ones are immediately released. The true way of playing the mordent is thus :

However, we adopted Rubinstein's way without comment.

What I have written about Rubinstein and Bach's "Triple Concerto in D Minor" recalls to my mind an occasion when I played it with Mr. Boscovitz and Mme. Essipoff at the latter's last recital here, I think in the year 1876. When, at the rehearsal, we came to discuss the mor-

dents, Essipoff exclaimed : "I cannot play
those things ; show me how they are done."
After repeated trials, however, she failed
to get the knack of playing them, as, indeed, so many pianists do, so at the recital she omitted them and left their
performance to Boscovitz and me.     I
think the effect of the concerto was not
marred by the omission.     The incident
just related must not be construed as in
any degree a disparagement of Mme.
Essipoff's playing ; as an artist she belongs
easily in the first rank of women players,
and her style is charming.

In taking leave of my old book by
Marpurg I present a specimen of advice
which he addresses to pianoforte-students,
namely : "In regard to deportment and
manners [at the pianoforte], one should
take care to avoid making faces, bobbing
the head, snorting, twisting the mouth,
gritting the teeth, and all such ridiculous
things.     In the absence of the teacher, a
pupil who has fallen into such ungainly
habits can correct them by means of a
mirror placed in front on the music-rack."

The foregoing is as honest a translation from the German as I am able to make. During a half-century's experience in pianoforte-teaching I do not remember a single case among my pupils of one who stood in need of this advice.

### A SIGNIFICANT AUTOGRAPH FROM RUBINSTEIN

JUST before leaving Weimar I had asked Rubinstein to write in my autograph-book, and he immediately complied.

The theme, which he wrote in the key of E flat major, is characteristic of him. It is strong and has a vigorous upward movement. It suggests the young man just starting out in life, with the vitality and courage of early manhood. It is dated "Weymar, le 5. Juin, 1854."

I did not see Rubinstein again until 1873, the year of his visit to this country. Happening in his room one day with my book, the idea occurred to me of asking him to write in it again, under his former signature.   For some reason he was averse to doing so, but finally consented.   At a glance the second theme seems like the first, but on examination the difference will appear.   He has transposed the theme to E flat minor, and its character is entirely changed.   The young man has reached the summit of the hill and realizes that he is now upon the descent.   The allegro maestoso of former years has changed to an adagio, and, as Rubinstein aptly writes, it is "not the same."

An autograph written for me by Joachim Raff is also interesting.   On the night before I left Weimar, June 25, 1854, Raff and I had supper at the Erbprinz together, and as the evening wore on we somehow got into a heated discussion about *Zukunftsmusik*, taking opposite sides. However, as a matter of course, we made up before parting.   He had previously written his musical autograph in the book, but now he added a kind thought to speed me on my way, namely : "That he may live well, work well, and soon return to Weimar music.   Mitternachtscheide."

RUBINSTEIN, PADEREWSKI, AND
"YANKEE DOODLE"

NOT long before Rubinstein's departure
for Europe he wrote a large number of
variations on "Yankee Doodle," and
meeting me shortly afterward, he in-
formed me of the fact, and added : "I have
inscribed your name at the head of the
title-page, and they are now in the hands
of the publisher." He said further, and in
a seemingly apologetic tone : "They are
good, I assure you, and I have taken much
pleasure in writing them." He played
this composition at his farewell concert
in New York, and in point of fact the
variations were very well made ; but I
think that much of his playing at the concert referred to was improvised.

The second season Paderewski was here
I sat next to him at a dinner given just
after his arrival. During conversation he
said somewhat suddenly : "Mr. Mason, I
have just composed a fantasy on 'Yankee
Doodle,' and have dedicated it to you."

He looked at me, and thought he saw
a curious expression in my face,—although I was quite unaware of such a
thing,—and continued, "You don't like
it!" "Oh, I do," I protested, "and esteem the dedication as a great honor."
"I see you don't," he said. "Well," I
replied, "I already have one 'Yankee
Doodle' from Rubinstein, and was think-
ing that the coincidence of your dedicat-
ing me another was very curious, that is
all.   Let me explain to you that 'Yankee
Doodle' does not stand in the same relation to the United States as 'God Save the
Queen' to England, 'Gott erhalte Franz
den Kaiser' to Austria, or the 'Marseil-
laise' to France.   'Yankee Doodle' was
written by an Englishman in derision of
us."   I am afraid that my remarks dis-
couraged him, for he never finished the
composition.   He played it to me as far
as he had progressed with it, and it is
certainly the best treatment of the theme
I have ever heard.   He had given it re-
spectability, and, indeed, he told me that
he really liked the tune.

MEETINGS WITH VON BÜLOW

VON BÜLOW, who had been a pupil of Liszt a year or two before my time, would occasionally return to Weimar from his concert tours, and during these visits I became well acquainted with him. In certain ways he was a wonderful man. He had an extraordinary memory and remarkable technic. He was invariably accurate and precise in his careful observance of rhythm and meter by means of proper accentuation, and the clear phrasing resulting therefrom made up a good deal for the absence of other desirable features, for his playing was far from being impassioned or temperamental. His Chopin-playing always impressed me as dry, and his Beethoven interpretations lacked warmth and fervency.

I remember he once said to me : "Rubinstein can make any quantity of errors during his performance, and nobody is disturbed by it ; but if I make a single mistake it will be noticed immediately by every one in the audience, and the effect will be spoiled."

Personally, Von Bülow and I got along very well together. He always made kind inquiry for me when he met common friends in Europe, and he once presented me with an autograph of Brahms which he valued highly. The following letter he wrote me shortly after his arrival in this country, in response to an invitation to make me a few days' visit in Orange, New Jersey, where I was then residing.

BOSTON, October 21, 1875.

MY DEAR COLLEAGUE: I have just now received your kind note, and although I have not a single moment of leisure, I want to thank you and to tell you how happy I should be to meet you again after nearly a quarter of a century out of sight.

Alas! it is quite impossible for me to make you a visit before my arrival in New York. I must work very hard in spite of a bad health and a not at all Rubinstein-like constitution.

As this specimen of cablegrammatical shows, I am unable to express myself in your language without a heap of wrong notes in every line. It was but two years ago, when I made my first appearance in old England (much less sympathetic to me than New England), that I began to stammer the Anglo-Saxon idiom. Please kindly excuse the shortness and weakness of my reply.

Many thousand most friendly compliments from our common co-pupil Carl Klindworth,[1] whom I saw last summer in Tyrol; we often spoke of you.

> Yours most truly,
> HANS VON BÜLOW.

I know from what Von Bülow himself told me that he accepted philosophically the trouble between himself and his wife Cosima Liszt, and her subsequent marriage to Wagner. Soon after he arrived in New York, in 1876, I called on him, and during our conversation I broached the subject in a tentative way. I was not sure that his feelings toward Wagner were not so hostile that mention of the Bayreuth master would have to be avoided, and I thought it just as well to arrive immediately at a clear understanding of the matter.

"Bülow," I said, "you will excuse me if

[1] He was at Moscow, being first professor of pianoforte-playing at the Conservatory there.

I touch on a rather delicate subject. Of
course your friends abroad know just what
your present attitude is toward Wagner;
but over here we know little or nothing
about it. Perhaps you would like to en-
lighten me. I hope, however, I have not
touched on a painful subject."

"Not at all," he exclaimed. "What
happened was the most natural thing in
the world. You know what a wonderful
woman Cosima is—such intellect, such
energy, such ambition, which she naturally inherits from her father. I was entirely too small a personality for her.
She required a colossal genius like Wagner's, and he needed the sympathy and
inspiration of an intellectual and artistic
woman like Cosima. That they should
have come together eventually was in-
evitable."

### EDVARD GRIEG

On July 1, 1890, my daughter, sister-in-
law, and I were in Bergen, Norway, having just returned from a very pleasant
trip to the North Cape.

Being so near Grieg's home, an hour
and a half's drive from Bergen, and having received an invitation to visit him,
we presented ourselves at his "Villa
Troldhangen" in the afternoon. The day
was bright and lovely, and thus we saw
Grieg's place under the most favorable
aspect. Our reception by Mr. and Mrs.
Grieg was most hospitable, and we felt
immediately at home. After half an hour's
conversation, we all strolled through the
beautiful grounds, which in many places
are thick with trees and shrubs, while
here and there are clearings through
which the waters of the fiord shine bright
and clear. The wild flowers, with their
rich, brilliant colors, were especially attractive ; indeed, this is everywhere in
Norway an attractive feature.

Mr. Grieg is a man of high intelligence
and culture, and is thoroughly natural
and genial. I have very pleasant memories of our cordial reception and delightful visit.

RATES OF TEMPO—THE PRESENT TIME
COMPARED WITH FIFTY YEARS AGO

IN recalling Liszt's playing I cannot help
noticing the marked difference in modern
rates of tempo as compared with those
which were considered authentic fifty
years ago. This is noticeable in many
of Chopin's compositions, especially the
larger ones, such as the sonatas, ballades,
fantasies, etc., with all of which I am very
familiar, having heard them played not
only by Liszt in Weimar, but in other
German cities, and by artists of the
highest rank, many of whom were contemporaries and personal friends of Chopin.
They all seemed to adopt a certain rate
of speed, as if in conformity with the
composer's intention, and it was in agreement with my own intuitions. Dreyschock and Liszt had often heard the composer play his own pieces and must certainly have been familiar at least with
his rates of tempo. I was very close to
the Chopin day, having been in Germany
only a few months when he died. Two

of my teachers and nearly all of the
musicians I had met were his contemporaries and had heard him play his own
compositions.   I certainly ought to have
the Chopin traditions.

### ELECTROCUTING CHOPIN

THE question is, Should Chopin be played
in accordance with the spirit of the time
in which he lived, should his works be
played in the tempo in which he played
them, or, because electricity has brought
about so many changes and has enabled
us to do so many things much more
rapidly than formerly, should Chopin's
music be electrified, or, as it seems to me,
electrocuted?   I think there is a general
tendency to play the rapid movements in
Chopin, and, in fact, in all composers not
of the extreme modern type, too fast.   To
play these movements rapidly and give
the phrases with absolute clearness, one
must have such breadth, command of
rhythm, and repose in action that he can
put the tones together like a string of

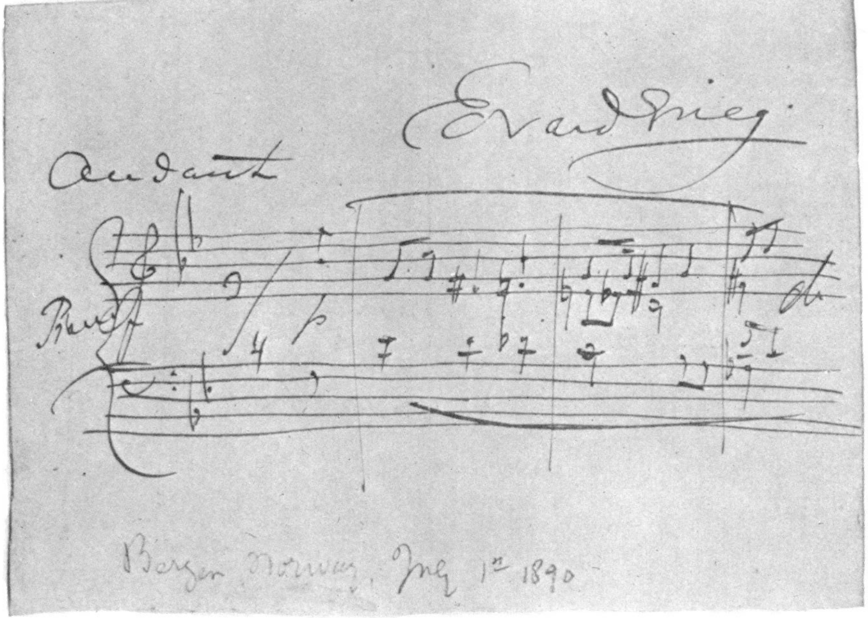
Andante
Edvard Grieg
Bergen Norway, July 1st 1890

pearls, so that each is rounded into shape,
and the phrase is a complete and definite
series of tones, and not like a lot of over-
boiled peas, so soft that they all mash
together.    In too rapid playing the effect
of speed is lost.    The Chopin "Waltz in
D Flat Major" is often played much too
fast.    The theme is said to have been suggested to the composer by a lap-dog in
his room suddenly beginning to chase his
tail.    Whether true or not, the story is
suggestive.    Destroy the contour of that
waltz by playing it at too high a rate of
speed, and the dog is no longer chasing
his tail, but dashing aimlessly about the
room.

Nor should the tempo be too slow.
Slow movements are effective, but sufficient animation must prevail to impart
life and fervency to the music.    A stream
may flow so sluggishly that the water
loses its clearness.    This is not repose, but
stagnation.    During the musical season of
1899–1900 in New York I heard modern
pianists play some of Chopin's compositions so slowly that the effect produced

upon me was like that of a music-box running down. One endures it for a while, but finally is wrought up to such a feeling of impatience as to induce the exclamation, "Either stop that thing altogether or wind it up."

### TEMPO RUBATO

In modern times there is also a tendency to excessive use of tempo rubato.

I have recently heard the second part of Chopin's "C Sharp Minor Scherzo"— the choral with arpeggio passages—played by a celebrated pianist in such a way that, mathematically adjusted, about one measure was added to every section of four.

The player was afterward highly extolled on account of his wonderful rubato effects. The truth is that he was all the while simply playing mathematically out of time. Rubato ("robbed") is a slight modification of rhythmic flow in alternation with a corresponding compensation; it is like excitement in verbal narrative;

it is alternately losing and making up, but within judicious bounds, so that in the end the balance is preserved. The nature of music is essentially "tune and time"—in other words, emotion and intelligence, or heart and head, in loving and well-balanced combination. These conditions are absolute and can never be violated without disaster. Hence a true rubato must be played in time, but accommodatingly.

### UNUSUAL PUPILS—TRANSPOSING— POSITIVE AND RELATIVE PITCH

I ONCE gave to an intelligent pupil the task of transposing one of Bach's inventions into various keys. My directions were that at her next lesson she should be prepared to play it successively in three or four different keys. As she came to my studio for her lesson but once a month, there was ample time for preparation, and she succeeded in accomplishing the feat with ease and without error. But, more than this, she continued her trans-

posing until she had completed the round
of all the twelve keys without a mistake
—a rare and creditable performance, de-
serving the emulation of all young ladies
and gentlemen engaged in the study of
musical development and the cultivation
of pianoforte technic.

Another case is that of a young lady
pupil not remarkably musical, but who
has an ear for positive pitch.  By this is
meant that she could immediately name
the pitch of any tone on hearing it sung
or played.  All competent musicians possess the power of relative pitch.  I mean
by this that if a definite pitch is given to
one who has a musical ear, the pitch of
any other tone immediately following or
sounding in connection will be instantly
perceived, and the interval between the
two tones—in other words, their pitch
relationship—at once understood.

The power of positive pitch has been
regarded by many as a very desirable
gift, but judging from the experience of
the pupil of whom I am writing, it would
appear to be just the other way.  This

THE STUDIO IN THE STEINWAY BUILDING—WEST SIDE

THE STUDIO IN THE STEINWAY BUILDING—EAST SIDE

young lady, to whom I had also given the
task of transposition into various keys,
complained, on coming for her next lesson, that the effect upon her was very
disagreeable, in fact, extremely painful.
She explained that she was obliged to
look at the music on the pianoforte-desk
while transposing, and that on account of
her quick perception of positive pitch she
heard in companionship both the tones of
the original key and those of the key
to which she was transposing, thus producing a jargon and discord which was
distressing.    This at first seemed very
strange to me, indeed almost incredible,
but not having an ear for positive pitch
myself, either by nature or through cultivation, I could not judge from personal
experience, so, having confidence in her
sincerity, simply gave her assertion cre-
dence.

Later on, however, her statement received confirmation through the authentic testimony of a German musician and
conductor of high eminence.    At the time
this gentleman came to our country,

somewhat over fifteen years ago, the
standard of concert pitch was slightly
lower in Europe than with us. Since then
it has been adjusted and is now uniform
the world over. This discrepancy caused
our German friend extreme annoyance,
for having an acute and delicate perception of positive pitch, it pained and confused him to hear the familiar symphonies
and other works of the great masters
played in a higher pitch than that to
which he had become accustomed. This
is, therefore, the penalty for an ear for
positive pitch.

Some of the greatest musicians have
possessed this faculty, notably Mozart, but
others of equal rank were without it. Of
course a musical ear of the most delicate
sensibility as to relative pitch is common
to all of them, and this by the grace of
God, as the Germans happily express it.

Another case is that of a lady having by
nature an ear for positive pitch, who
occasionally attends church with me.
She is constantly disturbed by the difference of pitch between the tones of the

organ and the pitch indicated by the
notes of the tunes in the  hymn-book.
She reasons that either the tones of the
organ are above standard pitch or else
the organist transposes the music.  At
any rate, the two vary by the interval of
a semitone.

Theodore Thomas is not only able to
detect the disagreement, but at the same
time perceives whether it is by reason of
transposition from the original key or on
account of the tones of the organ differing
from standard pitch.

### APPLEDORE, ISLES OF SHOALS

MY first visit to Appledore was in August,
1863, two of my brothers having discovered the island, so to speak, the year before.  We were enthusiastic fishermen,
and during our summer vacation almost
lived on the ocean.  Furthermore, during
almost the entire year I was engaged in
teaching or in public appearances as a
concert-player, so that in my vacation I
detested the very sight or even thought

of a pianoforte.   Appledore afforded an ideal retreat where retirement verging almost on oblivion was possible, and thus it happened that I had spent many summers there before my musical vocation was brought to light.

A few years later my friend Professor John K. Paine of Harvard University also discovered the Shoals, and from that time came year after year without intermission.   After a year or two he had a piano sent down from Boston for the summer and placed in the reception-room in Celia Thaxter's cottage.   I had the pleasure of Mrs. Thaxter's acquaintance, but up to that time simply in a formal way, and beyond a call on my arrival and one on taking leave, I had little association with her ; Professor Paine, however, quickly formed a habit of playing Beethoven's sonatas to her, and she very shortly showed a delight in music, and especially in Beethoven's sonatas, with which she became quite familiar.   In the year 1864 Isidor Eichberg accompanied my brothers and myself to the island, and that led,

still later on, to Mr. Julius Eichberg's
becoming an habitué of the island. He
brought his violin with him, and with Mr.
Paine frequently played compositions of
Bach for piano and violin. Finally I was
drawn into the current, and played, with
Eichberg, Schumann's and other sonatas.
As I grew older I gave less time to fishing.
Moreover, whereas I had formerly spent
only a couple of weeks or so at the
island, I now began to go early in July
and stay until September, so that in the
nature of things I could not fish all the
time, and gradually formed a habit of
playing in Mrs. Thaxter's cottage every
day from eleven o'clock in the morning
until the arrival of the boat, about an
hour and a half later.

Hers was an interesting and enthusiastic nature, which attracted to her many
literary and artistic people. She held, in
a most charming and informal way, what
may really be called a salon. The walls
of her parlor were covered with paintings
and pictures of all kinds, many of them
the work and gifts of personal friends.

As she herself expressed it, "a beautiful thought was always suggested whenever and wherever she looked."

Her love of flowers amounted almost to a passion, and no expenditure of time or strength given to garden work was grudged, even when the effort of very early rising was involved. And when did garden ever better repay the personal love and care of the gardener? Where were ever seen such radiant, waving poppies, such hundred-hued pansies, such stately and brilliant hollyhocks, and such fragrant sweet peas? And upon entering the parlor, it seemed as if one had hardly left the garden, so many and so beautiful were the masses of flowers.

As I have said, Mrs. Thaxter was very fond of music, and every morning welcomed those of her friends who shared this taste to hear any artist who might be on the island.

It was my pleasure, being so much at Appledore, to play a great deal in these informal ways. The doors wide open to the sun and salt breezes, the people sit-

ting in the room and grouped on the
piazza, shaded by its lovely vines, the
beautiful vistas of gaily colored flowers,
sea and sky beyond, made a charming and
ever-to-be-remembered scene.

Chopin and Schumann were the favorite composers, their compositions being
constantly requested. After a while I
enlarged the repertoire by introducing
several of Edward MacDowell's smaller
works. These found immediate favor.
Some half-dozen years ago, having become acquainted with and thoroughly
enthusiastic over the "Sonata Tragica"
of this composer, I began to play it
early in the summer on arriving at the
Shoals. At first the audience was somewhat reserved in the expression of an
opinion, but after a few hearings the composition found friends who really appreciated and enjoyed it. Being curious to
ascertain what result a closer acquain-
tanceship with the work would bring
about, and wishing to do some missionary
work, I formed the resolution of playing
it once a day during the season, and an-

nounced my intention to the audience. With but the exception of a few days, the scheme was carried out, and with gratifying success, for the "Sonata Tragica" became eventually the favorite of the majority, and it was constantly called for.

One or two ladies who found it tedious at the outset became thorough converts, and finally experienced genuine musical enjoyment from it. On the publication of the "Sonata Eroica" a few years later a similar result was reached, but not in the same degree as in the case of the "Tragica."

This incident is related to illustrate the remarkable effect of musical surroundings and the great advantage of living in a musical atmosphere. Here were people of intelligence and culture who, under adverse circumstances, would not have appreciated the beauty of these intellectual works, but who after closer association were led to perceive their beauty and who learned to love them.

Sundays were celebrated by the playing of Beethoven's sonatas. Every one seemed to look forward to and enjoy these pleasant mornings. Mrs. Thaxter was a delightful hostess, and possessed the rare quality of bringing out the best in those about her.

During the summer of 1894 Mrs. Thaxter seemed as well and active as usual, still working in her garden, still the lively center of her group of friends and admirers. One day she did not appear, nor the next, and then we heard she had peacefully passed away.

None who were at Appledore then will easily forget that 26th of August, nor the day she was buried on her island home.

The funeral service was held in the well-known sitting-room; the address was made by her old friend the Rev. Dr. James De Normandie, and, by request of her sons, I played Schumann's "Romance in F Sharp," and Dvořák's "Holy Mount,"

> The tides of Music's golden sea
> Setting toward Eternity.

When the simple service was over the coffin was followed by her old and faithful friends and the island fishermen to the grave by that of her father and mother. The long procession of people, through the gray mist, winding in and out along the rocky way, the leaden sky and sea, the hushed voices of the children, usually ringing out so merrily from rocks and hotel piazzas, accentuated the sense of our loss.

At the grave, all lined with bayberry and flowers, the coffin was lowered, and each of those present came forward and laid upon it a few of the flowers she loved so dearly.

## MUSIC IN AMERICA TO-DAY

A YEAR or two ago a young lady came
to my studio and asked for a single
lesson. She told me that she had been
studying in Germany for some years, and
named the city, which is one of the well-
known musical centers. She was then
going to the West on her way home, and
stopped a day over in New York expressly
for a lesson from me. I heard her play
several pieces, and was surprised and
pleased with her manner and style. She
phrased with intelligence and gave due
attention to rhythmic requirements. Her
tone was large, full, and musically resonant,
and could not have been produced otherwise than through the agency of the
upper-arm muscles, which were constantly in active use. The flexibility and

elasticity of hands and wrists were also apparent, and finally the evident repose in action of all of these qualities capped the climax. I said to her : "My dear young lady, I cannot add to your playing, for it is already finished and artistic. I might possibly suggest a different rendering in certain parts, but, after all, this would amount only to a matter of taste. If you had studied exclusively under my guidance for a course of years, and I had succeeded in doing my best, aided by your own intelligence and careful practice, I should have sought to bring about just the result which you have reached. I think your teacher must be a young man." "He is," she replied ; "but why ?" "Because," I answered, "his method is free from the stiffness and rigidity of the old German school. Has he, perhaps, a method of his own ?" Her immediate reply was, "He uses your method." She also told me her teacher's name, which I have now unfortunately forgotten. I think this teacher deserves to have more pupils !

But the time has gone by when it was necessary for students of the piano to go abroad to complete a musical education. There are now teachers of the piano of the first rank in all of our principal cities, who secure better results with American pupils than foreign teachers do, because they have a better understanding of our national character and temperament. Such men among my own former pupils are E. M. Bowman in New York, S. S. Sanford in New Haven, W. S. B. Matthews and William H. Sherwood in Chicago, and many others who are distinguished in their profession as teachers, and who have done and are doing much in furtherance of sound musical education and in the cultivation of a refined musical taste in America. Our country has also produced composers of the first rank, and the names MacDowell, Parker, Kelley, Whiting, Paine, Buck, Shelley, Chadwick, Brockway, and Foote occur at once to the mind. Enormous progress in the art and science of music has been made in America since I began my studies in

Germany in the year 1849. Our teachers meet in great numbers in convention during the summer months and in summer schools and classes, and it is difficult to overestimate the beneficent results which flow from these assemblies. They create a musical atmosphere, in which teachers and pupils live and move and have their being. They afford opportunities for the intelligent discussion of mooted questions and for the interchange of ideas, and lead to a wider dissemination of the best educational methods.

Harvard, Yale, Columbia, and Princeton all have their chairs of music, and doubtless this is true of others of our universities and colleges. The city of New York has become one of the great musical centers of the world. The Philharmonic Society, the opera season, the Kneisel Quartet, and many others of high artistic merit, afford opportunities for the gratification of musical taste which are hardly to be excelled elsewhere ; and the popularity of these and of the countless pianoforte recitals and chamber-music concerts bears

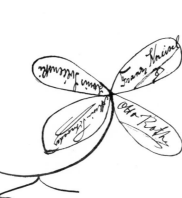

Unserem hochverehrten Gönner
Dr. William Mason
in aufrichtig empfundener Werthschätzung

New York. 4. April 1899

Franz Kneisel

Louis Svečenski

Otto Roth

Hans Schroeder

Kneisel Quartett

eloquent testimony to the growth of an intelligent musical taste among us. Boston and Chicago have their world-renowned orchestras, led by Gericke and Thomas, who are passed masters of their art. The cities of Pittsburg, Cincinnati, and St. Louis have their orchestras, each under competent leadership. The most celebrated artists at home and from abroad are heard in our principal cities. The season just closed (1900–01) is in striking contrast to those of my early manhood. Among the many prominent pianists who have played to us there are some of extraordinary talent, who give abundant promise of brilliant future achievement.

Ernst von Dohnányi, born at Pressburg, July 27, 1877, is a wonderfully talented musical composer and at the same time a pianist whose technic is complete, combining as it does the emotional, intelligent, and mechanical elements in happy union and adjustment. Von Dohnányi has by nature as intense, thorough, and complete a musical organization as

ever came within my experience. He
composes with marvelous spontaneity and
rapidity. His ideas are fresh and original,
and their expression and elaboration are
effected with the freedom of an improvisation, thus in no way emphasizing their
mechanical setting forth.

He is just completing, in the twenty-
fourth year of his age, an elaborate symphony in D minor for grand orchestra,
the scheme of which is as follows: I.
Allegro; II. Adagio; III. Scherzo; IV.
Intermezzo; V. Finale: Introduction,
Tema con Variazioni; Fuga.

This is a massive production, apparently the result of inherent qualities carried into act by impulse, in other words,
of spontaneous achievement. It is so instinctive and impulsive that the art of
its construction hardly occurs to the
hearer at first, but as an afterthought
excites wonder and admiration.

Early in March of the present year
(1901), Von Dohnányi, his wife, and a few
other friends, among them Emil Pauer,
dined at my house, and during the even-

ing Von Dohnányi played his symphony
on the pianoforte.    This instrument is
naturally quite inadequate to the interpretation of such a work, but Von Dohnányi's technic is so complete, his tone so
massive while intensely musical, and his
enthusiasm so contagious that we became
conscious of an ever-increasing interest,
steadily growing in intensity.    The occasion and its experience will not be forgotten by any of those present.

A week later the Von Dohnányis spent
the evening with us just before their departure on the following day for Europe,
and he played again a portion of the
work, deepening and confirming the impression made at the first hearing.    The
future of this young man is full of promise.    His teacher in composition was Hans
Koessler in Pesth ; his pianoforte teacher
was Stephen Thomán of the same city.
Later on he had eight lessons of Eugen
d'Albert in Berlin, after which the latter
said to him : "You can go on by yourself
now ; I have taught you all I can."

Leopold Godowsky is a pianist of the

first class, but above all he is a specialist,
and altogether unapproachable in his
specialty. His left hand is in every re-
spect the equal of his right, and passages
of extreme intricacy and rapidity come
out with an astonishing clearness of detail. Nothing in his work, however mi-
nute, is slighted, but musical expression
and finish of execution are above criticism. His specialty is his rearrangement
and working up of many of Chopin's
Études in such manner that several of the
various themes of these are, so to speak,
intertwined. In some instances three
different melodies can be heard progress-
ing simultaneously in loving union, with
a smoothness, delicacy, and accuracy in
counterpoint which is simply marvelous.
There is never a suspicion of haste in his
playing, no matter how rapid the rate of
speed. His manner is full of repose—
respectful, earnest, and sympathetic ; thus
there is no suggestion of violence to the
composer's original production.

I know that among my best friends,
whose judgment I esteem, there are some

who do not hold the same opinion, and who think that the composer's work should be left intact. It seems to me, however, that much depends upon the manner of treatment. The French proverb runs: "Il y a fagots et fagots"; or, in the more homely phrase of dear old Boston, "There are beans, and then there are beans." Moreover, the fact that these compositions are études (studies), and therefore avowedly for the purpose of developing physical technic as well as poetic style, should be duly considered in judging of their *raison d'être.* Similar treatment of the sonatas, ballades, and nocturnes would surely be a different thing. Furthermore, the solid and dignified Brahms—one of the three B's of Bülow's trinity—set an example, by rearranging a rondo by Von Weber, which he turns upside down, so to speak, making a bass of what in the original is the right-hand part. Brahms has also utterly destroyed the charm of Chopin's "Étude in F Minor, Op. 25, No. 2," which lies in the very rapid and delicately pianissimo playing of passages of triplets in the right hand as against duals in the left. In the original these passages are throughout of single tones in both hands, and hence can be performed in the most dainty and fascinating manner ; but Brahms has changed the right hand part to double thirds and sixths, thus completely altering the character of the music, and doing violence to the exquisitely light, delicate, and graceful effect of the original version. In passing judgment upon the work of Brahms, however, it must not be forgotten that he publishes this in company with several other arrangements, under the general title, "Studien für das Pianoforte," thus indicating that his object is the development of physical technic.

In this connection, I remember Rubinstein's telling me as long ago as 1873, in the artists' retiring-room during one of his recitals at Steinway Hall, that he used in his boyhood's days "to do all sorts of things with Chopin's études," as he expressed it, "in order to exercise and strengthen the fingers." By way of illustration, he went to an upright piano which happened to be in the room, and began playing with his left hand alone the right-hand part of the chromatic-scale étude, "Op. 10, No. 2," and this he did with fluency.

Godowsky has played his arrangements to me on several occasions at my studio and at home *en famille*, and has invariably produced a state of happy good humor which was of long duration and which in large measure returns to me as I write.

April 20, 1901. Yesterday evening I attended the farewell concert of Ossip Gabrilowitsch, the talented young Russian pianist. He was at his best, and proved his right to stand in the front rank of modern pianists. His playing throughout of a program of compositions of Beethoven, Brahms, Chopin, and Liszt was masterly, combining as it did genuine musical quality, intelligence in phrasing, and great brilliancy, as well as poetry in interpretation. He is yet a young man and has not reached the full climax of his power, and will doubtless show still fur-

ther development in the next few years.
Other pianists who have played in New
York during the season of 1900–01, and
who deserve to be classed with the highest, are Harold Bauer, who has deservedly
won a very high reputation through his
splendid ability in all styles of piano music, and Arthur Friedheim, whose recent
concert was brilliant in high degree, and
who on that occasion gave an interpretation of Liszt's great "Sonata in B Minor"
which it seems to me was not surpassed
by the master himself—and I have heard
Liszt play this work many times. Richard
Burmeister also gave a masterly interpretation of this same sonata earlier in
the season.   This is the sonata, by the
way, of which mention has been made, in
the earlier part of these "Memories," as
having been played by Liszt on the occasion of the first visit of Brahms to Liszt,
in the year 1853.

We have also had Teresa Carreño, Adele
aus der Ohe, and Fannie Bloomfield-Zeis-
ler, all of them of the first rank and established reputation.   Of these the first-

named is a friend of long standing, for my
first acquaintance with her dates back to
the early sixties, when she first came to
New York as a child prodigy.    I well
remember the impression she made upon
me at that time, both from her artistic
playing and her charming appearance in
short dresses and "pantalets," the fashion
for children of that day.   A friendship was
immediately begun and established, which
still continues.

Josef Hofmann, with his tremendous
technic and executive skill, has given
pleasure to many ; and Arthur Whiting,
Howard Brockway, and Henry Holden
Huss have ably upheld the reputation of
American virtuosos and composers.

In bringing these papers to a close, I
desire to make my grateful acknowledgment to the friends and pupils of many
years who united in celebrating the seventieth anniversary of my birth by presenting me with a beautiful silver loving-
cup, which I fondly cherish as an evidence of affectionate regard, and which
will be ever filled and overflowing with

loving memories, not alone of those who united in the gift, but of the many others whom I have known in the course of an unusually long professional career.    To one and all I offer my heartfelt thanks.

APPENDIX

# Part I

## EARLY LIFE OF LOWELL MASON

ADDRESS OF WILLIAM S. TILDEN, PRESI-
DENT OF THE MEDFIELD HISTORICAL
SOCIETY, AT CHENERY HALL, MED-
FIELD, FRIDAY, JANUARY 8, 1892,
THE CENTENNIAL ANNIVERSARY OF
THE BIRTH OF DR. LOWELL MASON

FELLOW-CITIZENS : Most that has been
hitherto said and written has been rather
concerning the public and professional
career of Dr. Mason ; and we shall doubtless have presented many interesting
mementos to-day, in letter and address,
relating to those things in which he is
most generally known.  What I have to
present in this paper will refer particularly to his birth, parentage, and early
surroundings, of which comparatively little has been said.

Lowell Mason was of English descent, being in the sixth generation from Thomas Mason and Margery Partridge. Thomas, born in England, was the son of Robert, who settled in Dedham, from whence he, with his brother Robert, came to Medfield in the second year of its settlement. The marriage of Thomas Mason and Margery Partridge, April 23, 1653, is the first recorded marriage in this old town. He received his house-lot by original grant from the town. It was upon North street, where Amos E. Mason now lives, the homestead having never been out of the possession of the Mason family. Thomas Mason and two of his sons were killed by the Indians on that fateful morning in February, 1676, when the town was burned. His eldest son was killed the following year, while fighting the Indians at the "Eastward" (now Maine), leaving one boy, Ebenezer, who was seven years of age only when his father was killed, and who, therefore, became the progenitor of the line from which Lowell Mason sprang. The son of

LOWELL MASON

FROM A DAGUERREOTYPE

this Ebenezer, Thomas Mason, left the homestead on North street, and settled in the extreme northeast corner of the town, at what is now known as the Charles Newell place. He married the daughter-in-law of Samuel Sady, who kept a tavern on North street, where the Pfaff mansion now stands; and his son Barachias, grandfather of Lowell, inherited, through his mother, that place, and settled upon it, where he lived with his son Johnson, father of Lowell. There the man whose nativity we celebrate to-day was born. The building has been preserved, and is, no doubt, the "farm-house," so called, on Adams Avenue.

The first twenty years of his life were spent in his native town of Medfield; and very little has ever been written about this portion of his life, and much of that somewhat incorrectly. His biographers seem to have endeavored to add to his fame by magnifying his want of opportunities for education and culture in his youth. In a discourse upon Mr. Mason's life and labors, the Rev. George B. Bacon, his pastor, says : "Mr. Mason had no advantages of education. He was the son of a mechanic in a small New England town. He began almost in his cradle that fight for a living which left small opportunity for study or culture." Another writer says : "He spent twenty years of his life doing nothing but playing upon all sorts of musical instruments, and there was no one to teach him their use." We feel inclined to believe that these statements were half-truths only, and are not a complete statement, by any means, of the conditions and pursuits of his youth.

We think it can be shown that while Medfield is proud of having such a son, he was fortunate in having such a birthplace. We believe in the influence of heredity in genius, but also in the influence of environments. He was especially favored in both these respects, descending for generations from an honored ancestry and surrounded in his youth by educated people of high moral and religious character. His parents were in fairly comfortable circumstances, and he was, as is

usual in such cases, permitted considerable freedom in following the promptings
of his natural genius, which, springing
as he did from a musical family, early
showed tendency toward that branch of
art.

Dr. Holmes says : "If we wish to edu-
cate a boy properly, we must begin with
his grandfather." Barachias Mason was a
graduate of Harvard University in 1742,
but one hundred and fifty years ago. He
was a schoolmaster, a teacher of singing-
schools, and a selectman of the town for
several years. This certainly is a fair
start, on Dr. Holmes's principle. His son,
Colonel Johnson Mason, Lowell's father,
lived with him, and inherited the homestead, where he kept a public school for
many years. He was a merchant. In
this pursuit, it seems, young Lowell assisted him in his boyhood, as we learn
that, on the occasion of his narrow escape
from drowning in 1806, he was out with
a team on business for his father, near
what is now poor-farm bridge, where he
was rescued from a watery grave by two

boys about his own age after having sunk
for the third time. Colonel Mason man-
ufactured straw goods to some extent.
He was also an ingenious mechanic, in-
venting some useful machines used in the
straw business of those days. He was
town clerk for nineteen years, town trea-
surer, and a member of the legislature ;
he was a musician, a player on musical
instruments, particularly the violoncello,
and, together with his wife, sang in the
parish choir for more than twenty years.
When the musical talent of the town
united, on a Fourth-of-July occasion in
1840, to supply the music, Colonel Mason
stood at the head of the basses, although
then over seventy years of age. He was
also a prominent military man, commis-
sioned captain in 1800, and lieutenant-
colonel in 1803. It will thus be seen that
he was one of the most intelligent and
influential men in the town.

So much for the parentage ; now for the
neighborhood influences about the Mason
family. The nearest neighbor was the
Rev. Thomas Prentiss, minister of the old

parish church from 1770 to 1814, and who
sent four boys to Harvard College, one
of whom was of Lowell Mason's own age,
a schoolmate and playmate. His seatmate
in the North School, which he attended,
and a lifelong friend, was the late Joseph
Allen, D.D., of Northboro, Massachusetts,
who ever said that Lowell Mason was one
of the best scholars in the school; and
the schools of the town being then under
the supervision of Dr. Prentiss, they were
doubtless fairly good schools. Ellis Allen,
another friend and schoolmate, said that
Lowell Mason was the most popular and
talented, as well as the handsomest, young
man in town. The next neighbor on the
other side was George Whitefield Adams
(brother of the celebrated historian, Han-
nah Adams), who built organs at his
homestead, where Dr. Bent now lives;
and, without doubt, Lowell was familiar
with that instrument, as he was with
many others — the violin, violoncello, flute,
and clarinet particularly. He led the Medfield Band in his day, playing the clarinet.
Mr. Adams went to Savannah in 1812,

accompanied by Nathaniel Bosworth of
this town, and young Mason went with
them, journeying the entire distance with
horse and wagon. Another near neighbor was Amos Albee, a schoolmaster and
musician of some note in those days,
author of "Norfolk Collection of Church
Music." He assisted Mason in his musical studies, as reliable accounts inform us.
Libbeus Smith, a relative of the Mason
family, was also a singing-master here
during the early years of this century.
James Clark, a fine player on the violin,
lived in Medfield in those days. From
these facts it is easy to determine that,
though the musical advantages of the
times would not perhaps satisfy the de-
mands of modern culture, yet the place
was by no means devoid of influences cal-
culated to encourage the special development of a young man musically inclined.

Lowell Mason commenced teaching
singing-schools when only a boy. He led
the parish choir when about sixteen years
of age, and conducted the music at the
ordination of Dr. Ranger of Dover in

1812, writing an anthem for the occasion, aided, it is said, by his neighbor Amos Albee. The Medfield Choir assisted at these ceremonies, Mr. Ellis Allen and his wife, from whom this account is obtained, being among them on that day. Lowell's two brothers, Johnson and Timothy, were also good musicians, and remained prominent in the church choir, both socially and instrumentally, for many years after he left Savannah. They became musical leaders in Cincinnati and Louisville. The old choir in those days was large, and it was made up from the most influential people in the town, which is an excellent thing for a church choir. The following are some of those who were members of it while young Mason took charge of the music: his father and mother, with his two brothers above named; Major Fiske, father of the late Captain Isaac Fiske; Captain William Peters, grandfather of Mr. William P. Hewins; Captain Wales Plimpton, father of Deacon G. L. Plimpton; Oliver Wheelock, a merchant of the town; Amos Mason, father of A. E.

Mason; Ellis Allen, father of the Allen brothers, from whose reminiscences we gather many of these facts. The old choir, it will be seen, was highly favored, in a military point of view, having a colonel, a major, and two captains. Mr. Mason often said, in after years, that there was more musical talent in Medfield than in any other town of its size in the State. This we can with confidence believe.

It is not, therefore, strange, with his inherited tastes and capacities, and surrounded as he was by musical people, that he should devote much of his time to music. It was his common practice, tradition tells us, to play from the meeting-house steps, summer evenings, upon the flute or clarinet, to the young people who would congregate around the locality—in this way, doubtless, doing much to contribute to the growth of a musical taste among the companions of his youth. The atmosphere of liberal culture which characterized his neighborhood aided him in taking a more intelligent view of musical matters, without which natural abili-

ties, and even special training, produce
comparatively meager results; and the
young person who knows nothing but
music cannot expect a very high place in
public estimation.

That he had much ability as a practical
musician is shown by the fact that when
he went to the South he was able to give
entertainments with his voice and violoncello alone, which brought him at once
to the front with the musical public in
Savannah; and his tact, executive ability, and intelligence gave him a position
as teller in a bank. About this time
the conscious purposes of his life were
changed, and the mode of life characteristic of his early years gave place to one
of deep-seated religious convictions. He
became a member of the Presbyterian
Church in Savannah, where he held the
position as director of music for many
years. He was also superintendent of
the first Sunday-school ever formed in
that city.

As an instance of his natural tact and
shrewdness, it is related of him that

while a resident of Savannah he under-
took the instruction of a new band that
was being formed somewhere in that re-
gion. On the first evening a considerable
number of instruments were brought in
with which he was unacquainted, and
some of them, even, he had never heard
of. He got over this difficulty by telling
the owners of them that it would be
necessary for him to take them all home,
that they might be "fixed and toned up."
When he brought them back, at the next
meeting, he had mastered them all, and
proceeded to give his instructions accordingly.

He had a remarkable degree of personal magnetism, which gave him that
wonderful control which he possessed
over classes and conventions. When he
taught or lectured, all eyes were upon
him, all ears were attentive, all wills were
moved by his. This, with his natural
aptitude for teaching, gave him the
prominence which he so readily won in
the chief cities where his mature life was
spent. Soon after his return to Boston,

about 1827, after fifteen years' sojourn in Savannah, he attained great popularity as a singing-teacher. He organized a class for the well-to-do ladies and gentlemen of Boston who wished to perfect themselves in music, the instruction to be by the new method, and gratuitous. Five hundred singers attended, and at the close voted him a bonus of five dollars each, or twenty-five hundred dollars for the term. He was in constant demand as a teacher and director, and it would be strange if those who had occupied the field before him, and who were now compelled to take a back seat or migrate to "fresh fields and pastures new," should not manifest some feeling of opposition. This he had to meet, in one form or another, during his twenty-five years' residence in Boston. The writers on musical matters during that period show very plainly that such was the case, often giving expression to personal feeling.

But as a teacher he had no superior, and but few equals, in this country ; and this not only musically speaking, but

pedagogically as well.  Horace Mann said
he would walk fifty miles to see him
teach if he could not otherwise have that
privilege.  Secretary Dickinson, of our
State Board of Education, says : "My first
notions of what good teaching is were derived from seeing Lowell Mason give a
singing-lesson " ; and this although our
honored secretary has no knowledge of
musical tones.  George J. Webb, one of
the best musicians in Boston, and himself
associated with Mr. Mason for many years
as a teacher in the Boston Academy of
Music, said that he had seen him teach
hundreds of times, but never without
astonishment at his wonderful power before a class.  Dr. George F. Root says that
he always became intensely interested in
listening to Mr. Mason teaching even so
simple a thing as the property of long and
short musical sounds.  The writer of this
sketch was himself a member of the Boston Academy of Music at its latest session
in 1851 ; and it is not too much to say that
he has never seen any one, from that day
to this, manifest such ability to hold a

large class of teachers and musicians to
the consideration of the topic under discussion.

He was employed by the State Board
of Education to teach music in the normal
schools and in the teachers' institutes for
many years. Through his influence singing was introduced into the Boston public
schools as a regular branch of study, which
occurred in 1838. He introduced into
this country the inductive method of
teaching singing, formulating a system
from the study of Pestalozzi and other
eminent European teachers. His system
to this day molds the instruction, to a
great extent, throughout the United
States. Modifications have been made,
but the principles which underlie all good
elementary instruction in music were un-
deniably first inculcated and placed before the people by him. He had, and
still has, a wide reputation ; but it is not
greater than his genius.

While we acknowledge with pride the
honor bestowed upon the town of his nativity, on the other hand, we think that

this "obscure New England village" is entitled to some credit for the formative influences which sent forth such a son. Some one has said : "The first great requisite to a man's amounting to anything is to be well born." He was born of the sturdy yeomanry of Medfield. We cannot but think that the influence emanating from the men, his neighbors and early counselors, who made the old town what it was a hundred years ago, and what it is even down to the present, contributes no little to the successful career of him whose centennial we celebrate to-day.

# Part II

## LISZT'S LETTERS

My dear Sir: It will certainly give me great pleasure to see and hear you again at Weimar, but I trust that you will excuse me if I do not accept the proposition you make, that of giving you regular lessons, from which, moreover, I fancy you would have little to gain.

As for your idea of settling for some time at Weimar, it would be well for me to discuss it a little with you before you carry it out. The distance from Leipsic being so short, it would cause you but little inconvenience to pay me a short visit here, in the course of which it will be easy for me to say exactly what I believe will be best for you.

Accept, my dear sir, the expression of my feelings of esteem and consideration for you.

F. LISZT.

WEIMAR, August 3, 1851.


DEAR MR. MASON: Your welcome letter gives me very hearty pleasure, and I beg you to rest assured of the continuance of my most affectionate feelings for you.

I often hear of your triumphs in America, and I rejoice to know that your talent is rightly appreciated and praised. Your compositions have not reached me yet, but I am all ready to make them very welcome.

In a fortnight I start for Weimar. The Tonkünstler Versammlung is to take place this year at Meiningen, from the 22d to the 25th of August. I shall attend it, as also the Wartburg Jubilee Festival, at which my oratorio "Sainte Elisabeth" will be given on the 28th of August. Perhaps I may meet there Mr. Theodore Thomas and Mr. S. B. Mills, of whom you

have spoken to me. The ability of Mr.
Thomas I have heard highly praised; I
have to thank him particularly for the
interest which he takes in my "Poèmes
Symphoniques." Those artists who desire to give themselves the trouble of understanding and interpreting my works
are separated, by that alone, from the
ranks of the commonplace. I, more than
any one, owe them gratitude, and I shall
not fail to show it to Messrs. Thomas and
Mills when I have the pleasure of making
their acquaintance.

The news which reaches me from time
to time of musical things in America is
usually favorable to the cause of the progress of contemporary art which I am
proud to serve and uphold.

It seems that with you chicanery, blun-
ders, and stupidity of a criticism perverted
by ignorance, envy, and venality, exercise
less influence than in the Old World. I
congratulate you on it. May you success-
fully follow the noble career of an artist
with industry, perseverance, resignation,
modesty, and an unshaken faith in the

Ideal—such as you showed in Weimar, dear Mr. Mason.

Your truly affectionate and devoted

FR. LISZT.

ROME, July 8, 1867.

DEAR MR. MASON: Mr. Seward has brought me your welcome letter and several of your compositions. These give me double pleasure, for they show that your time at Weimar has not been lost and that you continue to make good use of it elsewhere.

"L'Étude de Concert, Op. 9," and "Valse Caprice, Op. 17," are distinguished in style and of good effect. I can also sincerely praise the three preludes (Op. 8) and the two ballades, but with some reservation. The first ballade appears to me a trifle curtailed.

There is a certain something lacking at the beginning and toward the middle (page 7) which is necessary to make the *motif* stand out again, and the pastorale of the second ballade (page 7) figures there rather as padding—*embarras de richesse!*

And, since I am criticizing, let me ask
why you entitle your "Ah, vous dirai-je
Maman," "Caprice Grotesque"? Beyond
the fact that the grotesque style should
not intrude in music, this title does injustice to the ingenious imitations and harmonies of the piece which is otherwise so
charming; it would be more fitting to
call it "Divertissement" or "Variazione
Scherzose."

As to the "Method," you do not, of
course, expect me to make an exhaustive
study of it. I am much too old for that,
and it is only in self-defense that I occasionally try the piano—considering the
incessant fatigue caused me by the indis-
cretion of a crowd of people who imagine
that nothing can be more flattering to me
than to amuse them!

Nevertheless, in going through your
"Method," I find highly commendable
exercises, notably the *interlocking passages* (pages 136–142) *and all the accentuated treatment*  > > > >  *of exercises.*
May your pupils and editors derive thence
all the benefit they should.

A thousand thanks, dear Mr. Mason, and rely on my very affectionate and devoted feelings as of old.

F. Liszt.

Rome, May 26, 1869.


It will give me genuine pleasure to see you again, dear Mr. Mason. Next week I return to Weimar and shall remain there as usual till the middle of July.

Therefore, suit the time of your visit to your own convenience. I beg you to stay for several days at least.

A thousand affectionate and cordial greetings.

F. Liszt.

Vienna, May 23, 1880.

INDEX

# INDEX